On Sculpture
By
Leon Battista Alberti

Translated into English

With notes and commentary

By

Jason Arkles

On Sculpture

Leon Battista Alberti

ISBN 978-1-300-96585-5

Contents

Notes on the Text

Leon Battista Alberti was a gifted man who lived in an extraordinary time and place. Born in 1404, he was a generation younger than the group of artists and architects who within their lifetimes transformed art from its 'Gothic' mode to what we now call the early Renaissance. Donatello, Lorenzo Ghiberti, and Fillippo Brunelleschi are the giants of this generation upon whose shoulders stand Leonardo Da Vinci and Michelangelo. Sometimes working together, other times individually, these early renaissance artists applied their love of Classical arts and letters and scientific principle to more fully understand and master painting, sculpture, and architecture more than any had done since Antiquity. And Leon Battista Alberti was there to record it.

Often, Alberti is described as an early example of 'The Renaissance Man' – meaning he could do anything he applied his reason and talent to. He is regarded as a painter, poet, architect, sculptor, urban planner, and philosopher; it might be more apt to say he was a philosopher, writer, and theorist who sometimes painted, sculpted, and built. His great genius lay not in his talent in the arts, but in his ability to discern principle behind practice. He had personal friendships and relations with Ghiberti, Donatello, and Brunelleschi and many others, and was very well informed on their progresses in their respective fields. His great contribution was to theorize upon and explain these progresses in writing. Thus, On Sculpture.

There are two early versions of On Sculpture: one in Latin, titled De Statua, generally considered original, though whose exact date is uncertain – probably after 1443; the other in Italian, titled Della Statua and whose earliest version dates to about a century after the

On Sculpture

Latin, but is thought to have been written almost immediately after or perhaps even prior to the Latin text.

For a translation in English from the Latin text, there is Cecil Grayson's out-of-print translation of De Statua, which is published along with De Pictura. (There are several recent translations of De Pictura which do not include De Statua.) In Grayson's work you will find a scholarly, fairly accurate and concise translation, and in this academic sense, this present translation cannot compete. However, this translation has a different goal in mind.

My translation of Della Statua should not be considered a 'scholarly' translation. Instead, I treat it as the sort of work it was originally intended to be – a practical guide for understanding basic principles of sculpting. The Italian text, published by Cosimo Bartoli about a century after Alberti wrote De Statua, had the same goal in mind with his publication as I do with mine. Bartoli wished to bring the work into the vernacular of those most likely to benefit from it.

This is where Grayson's text falls short – not in terms of scholarship, but in terms of clarity of purpose and practical context. For instance, comparing Bartoli's text to Grayson's, Grayson translates "circulum" as "circle'. Bartoli's version records this as "le seste da fare il cerchio", or "the compasses for making circles", which, judging by the context of the paragraph, is what Alberti intended.

Thus, Grayson's translation reads "I ask you: shall carpenters have set-square, plumb-line, level and circle, with whose direction and guidance they can easily make the angles, and straight and even lines and surfaces, ..."

While my translation of Bartoli's work reads "Think about this: if the carpenters didn't have their squares, plumblines, levels and compasses, instruments by which it is possible to control angles and planes, ..."

If Bartoli's version is indeed a translation of the Latin, it is a fairly free translation, and this led Grayson and others to deride it as too loose and verbose compared to the original. From a scholarly, literary standpoint, that criticism is just. From the standpoint of a contemporary sculptor who wishes to absorb and utilize the advice and insight Alberti intended to offer, Bartoli's is the preferred version.

Speaking from the viewpoint of a contemporary sculptor, I wish to follow Bartoli's lead; I will keep my translation of Bartoli squarely in the vernacular of a practical guide or manual. I have completely reformatted the text; in previous publications the text was presented in its original format of a dozen or so enormous paragraphs. I divide the work into six sections which reflect the various topics covered by Alberti and the paragraphic phrasing is my own. In addition, I illustrate the text not only with the engravings to be found in various editions of Bartoli's text, but with photographs and illustrations which further clarify Alberti's principles and examples. Finally I offer commentary on the text as to the feasibility of Alberti's proposed methods, and how these methods compare to contemporary and historical practice.

When we read <u>On Sculpture</u> as a practical instructional manual, what stands out most is its theoretical, slightly abstract nature. We find several foundational principles related to rendering the human figure in sculpture, but these principles seem a few steps removed from his explanation of how one proceeds to sculpt. Alberti really wasn't more than a dabbler in sculpture; his interests were too varied and his temperament a bit too inquisitive, perhaps, to allow himself the years of practice it necessarily takes to fully understand the mechanics of producing sculptured work. When Alberti speaks of sculpture, it's with the voice of a perceptive and intelligent mind *imagining* the processes of sculpture, not with the voice of an experienced practitioner.

Indeed, Alberti's approach appears to have been to survey the practices of a blossoming art, identifying what he saw as underlying principles of that practice, and then to have presented that information in a concise form, with suggestions for improvements in practice based his discovered principle. That the results of his study were both effective and well-received by contemporary sculptors is a testament to Alberti's genius. That said, we have to take Alberti's writing on sculpture with several grains of salt, if we want to discover its value as a practical treatise.

We working sculptors must bear in mind, when reading Alberti, that On Sculpture's value does not lie in the instruction and use of various improbable contraptions for measuring the figure, or his canon of proportions: the real value is in the theory which underlies these devices and practices. The point of this translation is to highlight these principles and theories, some of which have been neglected in our day. A few principles and practices might be more familiar to those who lived and worked at the far side of the 20th century, before the near-demise of traditional figurative studio practice. Others have evolved over the centuries to become essential tools to the artist which remain widespread to this day.

Jason Arkles

On Sculpture

1. On the origins and nature of sculpture.

I think that the arts of those who wish to express and portray in their work a likeness, and the resemblances of subjects created by Nature, originated from this: that they by chance happened to see in some tree stumps, or in clay, or in various other materials, some features which could, with a little work, be transformed into something similar to faces made by Nature. They began therefore to ponder upon this, and exerted all diligence, and strove to see what they could add or remove, as they saw fit, so as to ensure there would not seem to be anything missing, and would appear almost real - a true likeness - and finish it to perfection.

Accordingly, by amending whatever this material required in its contours and planes, and by clarifying and refining, they fulfilled their desire, and not without much delight, surely. We should not wonder that as these men's studies advanced, they no longer needed to see an initial likeness within their materials in order to express any object they wanted; but some did it in one way and some in another, as not everyone learned to do this by a common rule or route.

On Sculpture

In the pursuit of perfection in their works, some added and took away, as do those who work in wax, plaster, or clay, whom we call modelers. Some others began by only taking away, and by removing that material which is deemed superfluous, they sculpt; revealing in the marble a form, or the potential shape of man, which was at first concealed. These we call Sculptors, brothers perhaps of those who carve into seals the features of faces once buried. The third kind are those who work by adding, like silversmiths, beating silver with hammers, stretching or extending it to the form they desire, always adding to it, in order to arrive at the figure they want.

There may be some who think that I number the Painters with this group, as they add color to their works; but if you ask them, they will tell you they strive to imitate the contours and tones of the subject in front of their eyes, not through the addition or removal of anything in their work, but in doing so through their own brand of artifice. But we'll speak of painters another time.

In truth, though they may go by different paths, each of these I have mentioned begins with this notion: to put in all their works to the best of their ability, the semblance of the natural and true products of Nature. In so doing this straightforwardly, researching and learning the correct and understood principles which we will describe, they will make many fewer mistakes, and their work will improve in every way.

Think about this: if carpenters didn't have their squares, plumblines, levels and compasses, instruments by which it is possible to control angles and planes, to direct and finish their work -do you think that in the end they could do it very easily and without errors? That sculptors might make so many excellent and wonderful works by chance, rather than through a firm method, and sure guidance, brought forth with a reasoned approach?

I resolve this: that in any art or discipline, one extracts from Nature certain principles, perfections, and rules, which if we examine them with care and diligence, and utilize them, we will undoubtedly do all we set out to do. And just as we have from Nature – in the form of a tree stump, or a piece of clay or other material, as mentioned – forms which beg us to transform it into what we see in it, Nature also shows us certain guides and certain means by which we may, with a solid step and sure principles, proceed as we wish. When we become aware of this, and desire it to be put to use, we can very easily and with great convenience reach the highest degree of this art.

Commentary - On the Origins and Nature of Sculpture.

Alberti begins his work by speculating on the manner in which the desire to sculpt might have arisen. The tone of the first few paragraphs is reminiscent of Pliny's *Natural History,* that informative and often hilarious summation of popular wisdom and lore of the Classical World. Alberti shared his passion for knowledge and the natural world with Pliny, who was somewhat of a role model for Alberti's writings and eclecticism.

But his speculative tone does not last long. Alberti's impulse for rationality and order imposes itself almost immediately, seeking to codify and define the art of sculpture and its practitioners. What's more, Alberti asserts that the practice of the art itself is governed by natural law – or put into contemporary terms, 'science'.

I resolve this: that in any art or discipline, one extracts from Nature certain principles, perfections, and rules, which if we examine them with care and diligence, and utilize them, we will undoubtedly do all we set out to do.

It is for this scientific exploration of artistic endeavor that Alberti is justly famous. His treatise <u>On Painting</u> is the foundational text for optical theory in painting, and presents for the first time the geometric codification of one-point perspective. We'll discuss both this treatise and theories contained therein later.

Alberti classifies sculptors by whether they create their forms by adding or taking away from their chosen material - a distinction often made in discussions of sculpture right up to the present day. Alberti adds metalsmiths as a third group. His discussion of the creation of figurative sculpture does not extend to the technical processes of firing clay or casting bronze when distinguishing various "modelers", but focuses on the materials involved in the initial creative act of rendering a likeness. This is misleading, however, as he talks of carving figures in marble as an equivalent initial creative act to modelling; in fact, sculptors in marble had been creating clay models from which to copy into marble for over a generation by the time he had come into contact with the craft. Alberti of course knew of this process; he mentions it in the third section. To be sure, direct carving into marble was still in practice, but the use of clay and plaster models for marble carving was one of the primary technological and procedural advances that distinguished early Renaissance sculpture from its Gothic predecessors.

2. The two principles of likeness.

Now, just what these guides given by Nature to the sculptor are, we need to explain. As sculptors take as their foundation the imitation of likeness - or put another way, similarities - we ought to start with likeness.

 I might here propound on the logic of likeness – that is, ask why is it always seen in Nature, that in any sort of animal, every one of its kind that is very similar to every other. But on the other hand one cannot find anyone in the entirety of men, so to speak, one who has a voice totally like the voice of another, or similar noses, or other parts, or any such thing. Add to this the faces we have seen of our children - when we have known them as little boys, and afterwards knew in their youth, and now we see as old, no longer recognizable as they were, their faces having changed from day to day so much, changing through time; we may declare that some things are to be found in bodily forms which, with space and time, become variable, while there are some natural and true forms that remain continuously stable and firm, and which persevere due to the similarity of its kind. Leaving aside other considerations, we will speak briefly of this, as it touches the subject with which we have begun.

The how and why, or the principles of taking a likeness as the sculptors do, as I understand it, are through two paths; one of which is that this likeness, or image, which we make of the animal (as a manner of speaking in reference to Man) will be as far as possible similar to Man. It doesn't matter that the likeness is more similar to the face of Socrates than that of Plato, or another man known to us. Such a work will be successful, if it looks like a man, even if he is unknown to us. The other principle is for those who want to represent not only the likeness of a man in general, but that of an individual, let us say that of Caesar or Cato, being in a particular way, with this particular dress, sitting in court or addressing the populace; laboring to imitate and express all the habits and attitudes of that figure, or any other person known to us.

These two resolutions or deliberations, to treat it as briefly as possible, correspond to two subjects, namely, dimensions and pointing. We shall treat each of these, what they are and what they do, to lead a work to perfection: but first I will describe what utility the sculptor has from them. For they really possess a wonderful, sure strength that is almost unbelievable. Because one who is instructed in these things can perceive and record, and make definitive notation, of the features, positions, and postures of the parts of any body; so that not merely on the day after tomorrow, but after a thousand years, he can at will replace that same body, established and located accurately, in precisely the same position and site in which it was found the first time: so that not the least part of that body is not placed back into its initial site and point in space.

Or if for example you were to stretch a finger to point at the star of Mercury, or the new Moon rising, but finding that point in space using the angle of the knee, or finger, or elbow, or some other similar thing; with my guides and methods one surely could do it, without, even the slightest of errors; you could be certain not to doubt these means.

In addition to this, if for example I had covered with wax or clay a statue of Phidias, to the point it had become a thick column, you could, with these aids and these rules, affirm with certainty where to pierce the column with a needle, to find the pupil of the eye, and touch it without doing any harm; and where to find the navel, and where the big toe is, and all other things like these.

On Sculpture

You arrive at this when you have certain information about all the angles, and all the lines and their according measurements, and where they run together; you may in either method of working from life or from a modello[1], not only portray or paint[2], but actually record in writing the lengths of the lines, circumferences of circles, the positions of the parts, in a manner you shall not doubt. Through these means and aids, you will not create anything other than a likeness to it - or a smaller one, or ultimately one of such greatness, even of a hundred fathoms; do not doubt, I desire to say, that you could not make one as big as Mount Caucasus, as long as these grand undertakings do not lack the means: and what perhaps you may marvel at still more, you can do half of this statue on the island of Paros, and the other half could be carved and finished in the mountains of Carrara: so that in joining them, and aligning all the parts, the whole body and surface of the image will knit together, and match the live model, or modello, from which it was to have been made.

And the principle and the means of doing all this you may have so easily, and is so clear and unimpeded, that in my opinion, I believe that one can commit errors only with great difficulty, except those made on purpose, or in experimenting, disobey what was said.

I have not said why I teach this artifice, by which you will be completely able to make all the universal similarities of bodies, or why one should learn to do it, and so portray any differences or similarities. I confess that I do not take up the profession of teaching in this way, for example: "Here is the manner in which you make the

---

[1] To avoid confusion between live models and clay models, I keep the Italian "modello" to indicate a clay model, or plaster cast (typically, copying into marble is done from plaster casts of clay models).

[2] "Paint" (*dipingere*) used here by Alberti to mean 'render'. Similar to the contemporary use of the Italian term 'disegno' to mean either the act of drawing or of composition (or both), Alberti also applied 'dipingere' to sculptors and the work of sculpting in his treatise On Painting.

expression and the face of Hercules while fighting with Antaeus, so that he represents as much as possible the skill and pride appropriate to him, versus how you give him a benign and cheerful and laughing aspect when he caresses his Deianira - truly dissimilar from the other expression - even if it is the same face of Hercules. Here is how it happens in each different body and in different figures and poses, the action of the limbs, and their postures, lines and details which are seen to terminate in one way in one who is on his feet, in another way in those sitting, and in another in those who are to reclining - and in other ways in those who turn, are bent towards one or the other hand, et cetera, etc." My intention is to discuss all these things; that is, the manner in which with firm, certain, and true laws, you can imitate and portray any of those attitudes.

Commentary - The two principles of Likeness.

The how and why, or the principles of taking a likeness as the sculptors do, as I understand it, are through two paths...

Sculptures which resemble humanity, Alberti argues, can be made either to represent mankind in a general way, or may represent a particular individual. Each type of representation has its usage and function, and each may require distinct methods. Here Alberti begins a conversation which has been taken up and continued for five centuries by artists and academics. In fact, the history of modern[3] European sculpture has been a tug-of-war between two aesthetic principles.

In one camp, which we might call the Ideal, we can generally lump together such movements and themes as Renaissance Classicism, Neo-Classicism, the 'Beaux Ideal', and even the Baroque; it is the province of allegory and metaphor; it is the voice which expresses Neoplatonic truths, Christian faith, and Enlightenment aspirations. It can deify a Napoleon and give flesh to a sin or a virtue.

In the other camp which for lack of a better term we might call the Real, we find the vehicle for love and death in Romanticism, the nobility of human endeavor in Realism, the celebration of the beauty of the physical world in Naturalism. It is the province of the portrait bust and the genre statue. It can record for posterity the emotional and psychological state of a contemporary individual; it can give voice to empathy and personal expression.

These two fundamental approaches to the figure and their inherent natures are of course not two opposing camps, but merely two ends of a spectrum. Thus Canova's Napoleon can be considered equal

---

[3] 'modern' in this sense signifies from the Renaissance forward, rather than the art movement known as Modernism.

parts portrait statue and Greek God; Francois Rude's Neapolitan Fisherboy we can appreciate for its simultaneous representation of Classic beauty, and of a boy at play.

But all this comes after the time of Alberti. In his typical, no-nonsense approach, Albert boils the question down to one of technique. How does one represent the Ideal? How to recreate the Real?

These two resolutions or deliberations, to treat it as briefly as possible, correspond to two subjects, namely, dimensions and pointing.

These two subjects – 'dimensions' and 'pointing' – will be described in detail in the following sections of Alberti's treatise. It's worth remarking here, however, that each of these methods of measurement of the human figure have been in use in one form or another since before the 15th century when Alberti wrote, right up to the present day. But Alberti distinguishes himself by regarding each technique as corresponding to fundamentally distinct modes of representation. He is in fact correct. 'Dimensions' is more or less the technique of working from a canon of proportions - a canon developed from taking the average of several models deemed beautiful, to arrive at an ideal. 'Pointing' is the transfer of measurements from an individual model to one's work, which allows for a close approximation of the actual individual model. It is common for contemporary sculptors to be unfamiliar with how a given technique provides a certain outcome; thus all too often one sees sculptors struggling to render a portrait bust by the use of proportional rules (dividing the head into equal parts with horizontal lines, a center line, making the head 'five eyes wide', etc).

I will describe what utility the sculptor has from them. For they really possess a wonderful, sure strength that is almost unbelievable.

On Sculpture

These "almost unbelievable" claims Alberti makes, while not exactly practical, are not exaggerations. The method of pointing is capable of everything Alberti states here. While it might be very impractical to write down on paper each and every measurement taken from an X,Y, and Z axis of every square millimeter (see the commentary on section 4) in order to record the form of a given subject, it is possible. What sculptors do in practice is simply transfer each measurement from the subject directly into the clay or marble, rather than write it down numerically; and then they do so only as much as it is needed to render the rest of the work by eye, rather than slavishly locating every square millimeter of the modello's surface. That said, the technology now exists that can indeed record *ad infinitum* these measurements. A modello can be scanned three-dimensionally and converted into coordinates to produce a copy in marble by a robotic, computer-controlled marble milling machine. Three-dimensional printing uses the same principle. This operation can indeed occur "not merely on the day after tomorrow, but after a thousand years". Similarly, these mathematical measurements can be multiplied and divided for enlargements and reductions, and different parts of the came sculpture may be made separately and assembled perfectly, as Alberti states.

3. On Dimension.

I have mentioned two guides, and these are the dimensions, and the setting of points. We will discuss in the first place the dimensions, which are certainly nothing more than a stable, firm, reliable and informative guide, by which one records in writing and measures character, proportion, and harmony, which all the parts of the body contain one relative with the other, such as height as regards thickness, carrying this through the whole length of the body. And this knowledge is made known through two things, and those are a great rule stick, and two mobile squares: we measure and take the lengths of the limbs with the ruler, and with the squares all the diameters of those limbs.

The length of this ruler is taken from the length of the body that we would like to measure, that is, from the top of the head to the sole of the foot. I point out that to measure a man of small stature one ought to take up a smaller ruler, and a man of great stature one ought to use a larger ruler- that is, longer. Regardless of the length of the ruler, we will divide it into six equal parts, and such parts we will call feet, and from the term feet we will call this ruler the ruler *del piede*. We divide then again each of these feet in ten equal parts, and these small parts we will call inches. It will be therefore that the entire length of this ruler is sixty of these inches. Again divide each of these inches in ten equal parts, and these small divisions I call minutes. From these divisions we will have the length of the ruler be six feet, equal to 600 minutes, and each single foot will be 100 minutes.

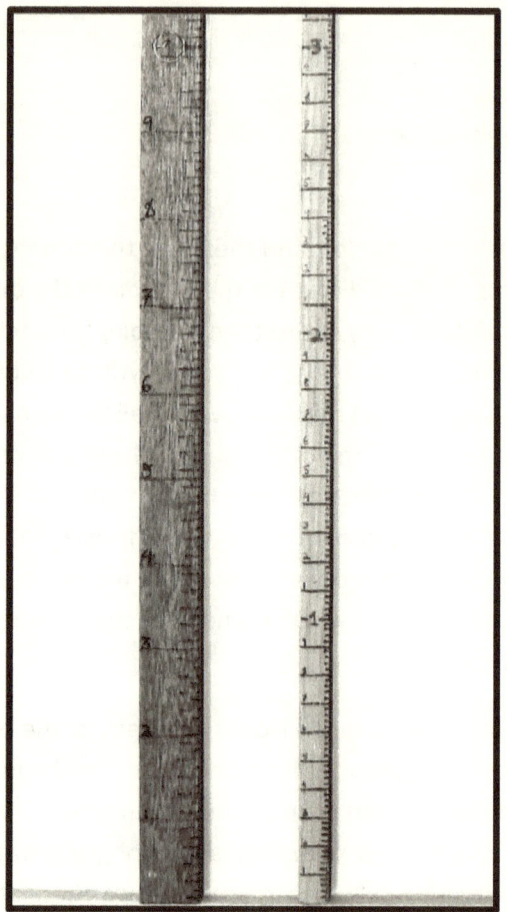

1. The ruler on the left has its units based on the height of a living model; on the right, the reduced version (3:1).

We will make use of the ruler in this way. If for example we would like to measure a human body, we will approach him with the ruler, and with it take note of every length of the limbs, from the soles of his feet up, and how much a part is away from another part, as for example, from the knee to navel, or the pit of the throat, or the like, how many inches and how many minutes. Sculptors should take this very seriously, and painters too, seeing that it is useful and very necessary, for knowing the number of inches and minutes of all the parts, we have the determination of these limbs expeditiously at the ready, such as that you cannot make any mistake.

Nor should you care to listen to the arrogant man who might tell you that this member is too long, or this is too short. See that your ruler will be that with which you make determinations and govern the whole work, for is more truthful than any other thing. And have no doubt that in examining these things well, that you yourself will become aware that your ruler is the source of countless other conveniences. It will be seen that you come into full knowledge of the way to establish and terminate your lengths in a smaller statue, and similarly, a still greater one. For if you had to do for a statue of 10 fathoms, for example, you'll have your ruler of 10 fathoms, and divide it into six equal parts, which corresponding together with the smaller ruler with its proportionately identical marks of inches and minutes, you'll see that its use, manner, and measurements will be the same as that of the other ruler. It will be seen that half of the numbers on the greater ruler, has the same ratio to its entirety, as half the numbers on the smaller one. And that is how you will need to make your ruler.

Now we have come to discuss the squares: we make two of them, one of which will be made in this way; that is, of two rulers ABC; we call the upright rule AB, and BC is what we call the base rule. The size of each of these rulers must be such that the base is at least 15 inches of its kind. By 'of its kind', I mean the same scale of inches that you have made in your ruler, according to the body that you want to measure; as I said above, a large ruler will have large inches, and in a smaller one, smaller. With these inches, then, made as you wish, mark on the ruler their marks and their minutes, starting on the base from the angle B going across to C, equal to the inches and minutes on the ruler. This square being marked in this way, as in the example ABC, we superimpose another identical square, called DFG, in a manner that the length of GF serves as a straight line and a base for both squares.

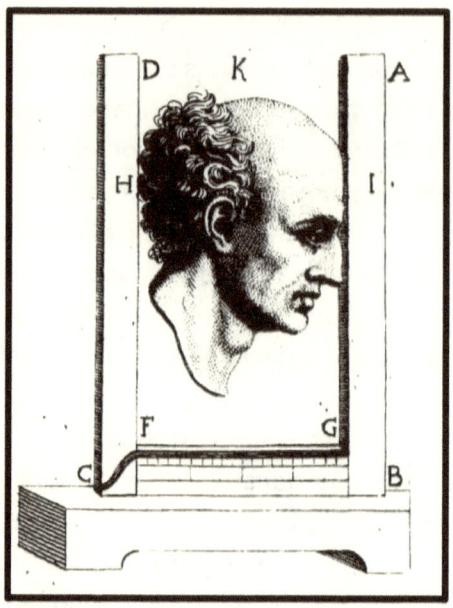

2. Alberti's squares, in the act of measuring the width of a human head from front to back.

Let us say I would like to measure the diameter of the thickness of the head AKD. Moving the straight edges of the squares - AB and DF - closer to or further away from the head to the extent that they touch the thickness of the head, ensuring the bases of the squares mutually form the same fixed and straight line. In this way, through the touching points of A and D, or rather the upright rulers of the squares, I will see what the diameter of this head is. And with this exact same method or rule I will take all thicknesses and widths of any member I want.

I could tell you many conveniences and many utilities that you can extract from this ruler and these squares, and if I did not think it was better to remain silent: with such things as this, any mediocre talent can by himself consider and understand the method to measure the diameter of any part, as would be for example if he wanted to know the diameter from one ear to the other, i.e. from right to left, and in what place it intersects with the first diameter, going from forehead to the nape of the neck, or the like.

Ultimately, if you take my word for it, and make use of this ruler and these squares, they will serve as faithful, firm and true guides and advisors, not only when working, but during initial preparation for work, so that you cannot find any part of a statue, no matter how small, which you will have to do that which was not already considered, examined, and made very familiar.

Here's an example: Who would dare to take up as their profession that of master ship builder, if he did not know what the parts of a ship were, and how one ship is different from another, - what sort of navy might we expect? And who might it be from among our sculptors, as they consider themselves, who could be asked: For what reason have you made this part in this way, or what proportion has it with this or that other part, or which is the proportion of this part to that of the whole body? Who will be the one to say they have been so diligent and careful, that they have noted and considered it all sufficiently or within reason, and as one expects from one who knows well the art they profess?

Undoubtedly, one learns the arts primarily through reason, principle, and experience. Never has there been any one that has made art as well as one could desire, if they have not first learned every facet of their art.

Commentary - On Dimensions.

Alberti's subject of Dimensions is nothing more than linear measurement of the parts of the living model's body, using two types of measuring devices. Simply put, if one wants to get the proportions, thicknesses and lengths of a subject correctly, one simply measures those proportions and lengths.

Alberti's instruction on constructing a ruler with units of measurement based on the total height of each individual model is quite interesting. At first blush this seems a needless hassle, living as we do in the age of standard units of measurement. If the sculptor is taking measurements to construct a modello of equal size to the living model, this would indeed be superfluous. However, for enlarging or reducing the scale of the work, Alberti's system is extremely useful.

For scaling down, Alberti calls for two rulers: one the total height of the live model, and one the total height of the reduced-scale, clay modello. Each is divided into six parts called feet, each foot further subdivided into inches and so on. The idea is that if a part of the body – let's say the arm – is measured at a length of two feet on the large ruler, the arm of the reduced scale figure will also have a measurement of two 'feet', as shown on the small scale ruler. No mathematics is involved in the scaling down of the measurements.

Now let's imagine a situation in where it is necessary to create a small figure to fit into a pre-existing niche. This reduced figure needs to be exactly thirty-five inches high. With Alberti's system, you make one ruler the height of the model, and the other ruler thirty-five inches tall; dividing both into six parts and so on. Like in the first example, what measures on the full scale at two 'feet' will measure on the small scale at two 'feet'. With Alberti's method, it is simple enough.

But if you were given the same task and chose to forego making the two rulers, and instead used a tape measure (Standard US Measurement, to drive the point further), this is what you would need to do:

First, you would measure the height of the living model – let's say five foot eight inches, or 68 inches. Then, you find the reduction to thirty-five inches as a percentage: 51.47%, so we'll call it 51.5%. That means for every measurement you take on the living model with a tape measure, you will have to multiply it by .515 to get the reduced measurement. Therefore, an arm measuring 24 inches (on the living model) will be reduced to 12.36 inches for the reduction; then convert that into a fraction: 12-9/25", and finally estimate the closest fraction on your tape measure: between 12-5/16" and 12-3/8". Not so simple.

Alberti's other measuring device – the moveable squares - are really just a set of calipers, which take measurements of width, as shown in illustration 2. Larger and made of wood, his are a bit unwieldy but will do the job. Some sculptors conflate the term 'compass' with 'caliper' – but these are two different devices, though they perform similar functions. Compasses are lighter, more maneuverable, and more available in Alberti's day than calipers, being a more common tool used by masons, carpenters, and others. But there is a good reason Alberti advises the use of calipers.

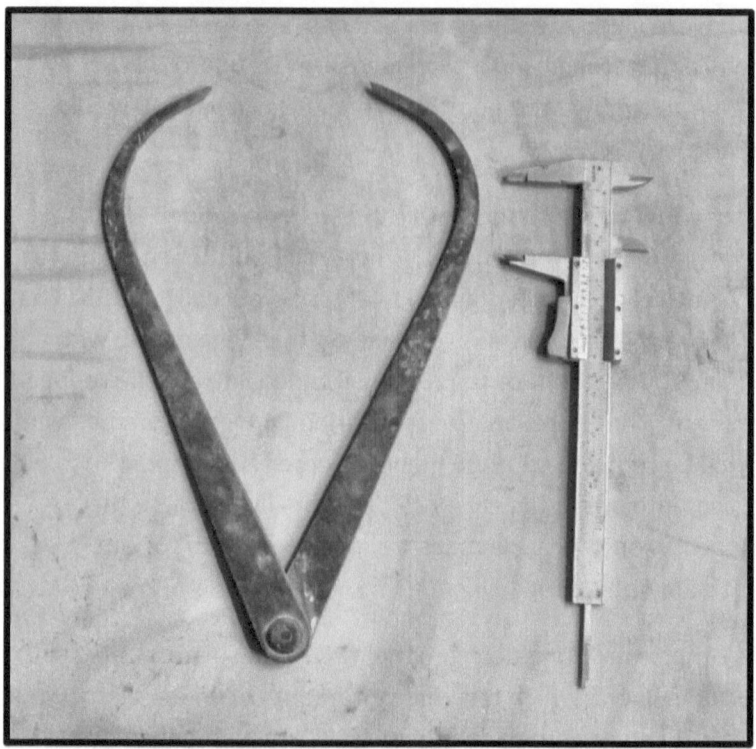

3. On the left, a set of compasses. On the right, a set of calipers.

The difference between calipers and compasses is that calipers take their measurements at the *maximum* width of an object. This is done by reducing the distance of the two arms of the calipers until both are touching the object being measured. Compasses can take the same measurement, but only if the location of the maximum width of the object is known beforehand. As seen in illustration 4, it is easy to slightly miscalculate the location of maximum width of something in cross section, say an arm, with compasses. With Alberti's mobile squares, it is impossible to take the measurement of anything BUT the maximum width.

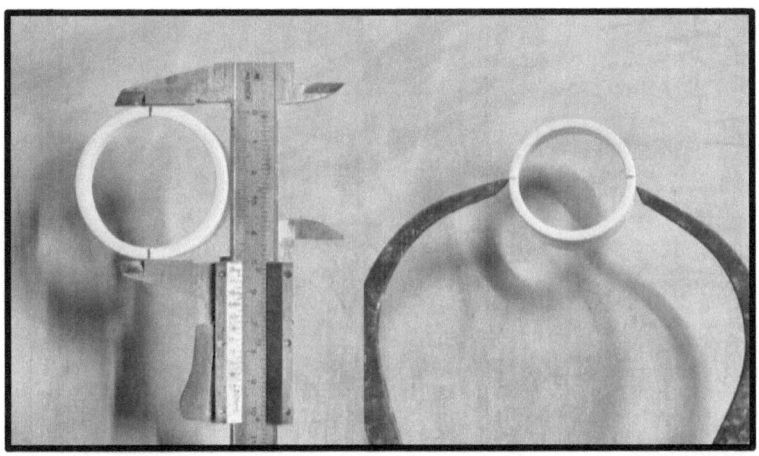

4. Left - Calipers recording the maximum width of a circular object, indicated by pencil marks. On the right, compasses also taking a width. Without the pencil marks, there is no guarantee the compasses will take their measurement at the true width of the circular object.

Compasses are certainly useful to the sculptor and are much more widely used by sculptors in contemporary times than calipers. They are useful in taking measurements from one definite point to another, such as from the corner of the mouth to the corner of the eye. They are also one of the most misunderstood and misused tools around. Alberti was wise not to bring them into the conversation, as their proper use is rather more complex than it would seem and leads many sculptors astray. Although compasses are perfectly suited to taking measurements from three dimensional forms, they provide a linear – that is to say, a two-dimensional – measurement. This means that unless the compass is being used to *triangulate* a given point from other points lying on different planes (Y and Z axes), a single measurement taken off a three dimensional form is often useless and misleading. This will be more fully discussed in the commentary of Section 4.

4. On the Setting of Points.

We have treated the dimensions, how one accurately finds them with the ruler and the squares: now it remains for us to discuss the setting of points[4]. The setting of points is the determination you make to draw and develop all the contours and determine angles, hollows, and projections, all located in their places with true and certain guidance.

 These determinations will be most excellent when taken from the center of a central point, using a plumbline to mark and record all the extremities of all the lines, down to the extremities of the figure. Between the dimensions spoken of earlier, and the setting of points, there is this difference: the dimensions underlie all, and provide us with certain things more common and universal, those which are more inherently fixed and stable in the nature of the body, such as lengths, thicknesses, and widths of the limbs; and the set points give us the momentary variety of limbs caused by new attitudes, and movements of the parts, and teaches us placement and location.

Therefore, to do this well, we need an instrument, such an instrument having three parts, or members, being made of a horizon, a boom[5], and a plumbline.

---

[4]'Porre di termini' or terminal points. In the Latin text Alberti calls it 'finito', and Grayson's translation of this leaves that term untranslated, for lack, perhaps, of a precise word in English. For the last few centuries, however, practitioners of sculpture have referred to the location of points on the surface on a modello as 'pointing'. The various devices used to take these points are referred to in general as pointing machines. The device and method Alberti describes is the grandfather of these.

[5] 'linda' in the Italian text.

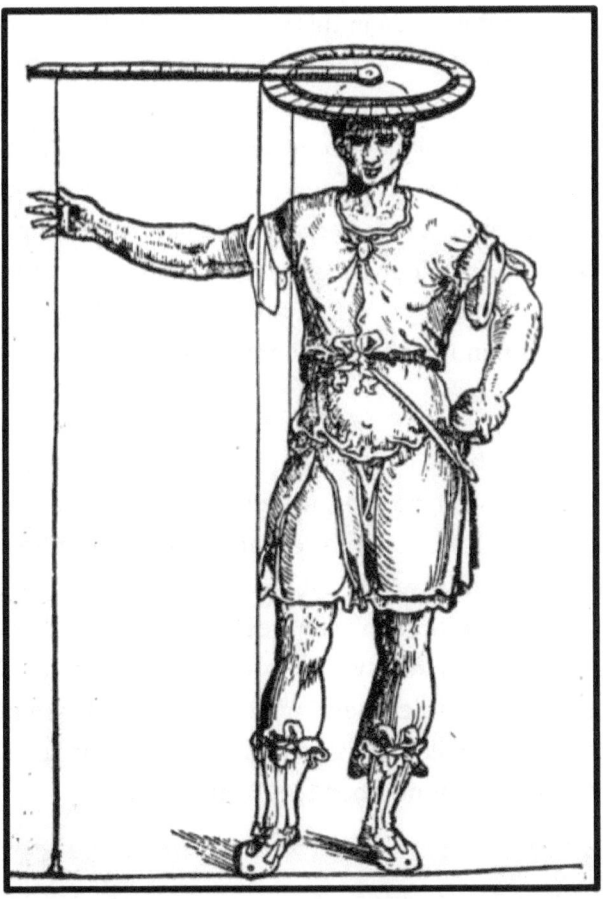

5. The Diffinitore mounted upon a statue. From the Claudius Popelin translation, Paris 1868.

The horizon is a plane upon which is drawn a circle, divided into three equal parts and marked with numbers. The boom is a straight rule, one of whose ends is fixed in the center of that circle while the other revolves at will, by which you may align it to each of the divisions made in the circle. The plumbline is a straight wire or line that falls squarely from the top of the boom to the floor upon which rests a statue or a living figure, upon which you have to fix the points of the parts, and aforementioned linear measurements.

On Sculpture

And this instrument is made in this way: take up a flat board, well planed and clean, and in that take a circle, the diameter of which is three feet, and the circumference of said circle, at its extremity, is divided in equal parts , similar to those which the astrologers draw on astrolabes: these parts I call degrees. Each of these degrees I divide again in as many other parts I would like, for example, each one is divided into six minor parts, which I call minutes, and to all these I assign a number, i.e., 1,2, 3, and 4, etc., until I have numbered every minute. This circle, thus made and numbered, is called a horizon.

To this circle I attach the mobile boom, which is made in this way: I look for a thin and straight ruler, the kind three feet long, and one of its ends I attach with a pin to the center of the circle or horizon, in a sturdy manner, but in a way that it can turn, and the other end coming off the rim, so that you can freely transpose and rotate it all around. On this boom I mark with those inches we are familiar with, similar to those of our ruler mentioned earlier. And these inches I divide yet again in smaller parts, as was done with the ruler, and starting from the center number 1, 2, 3, and 4, etc.

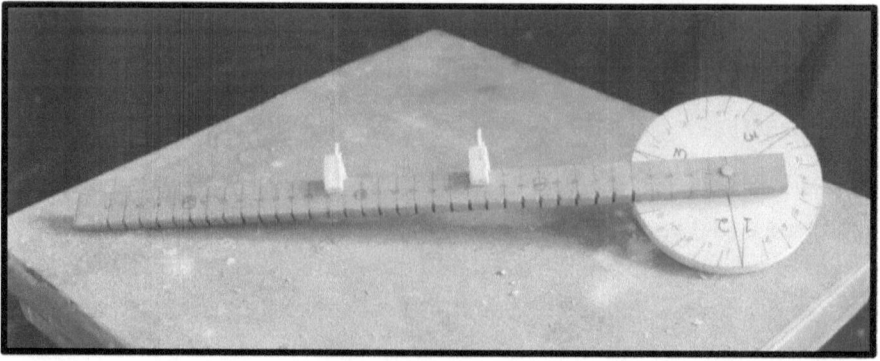

6. A Diffinitore made for a small scale figure. The pegs along the boom are for hanging plumblines.

To the boom I attach a thin wire with a little lead weight: and this entire instrument made of the horizon, the boom, and lead, I call the Diffinitore[6], and it is as I have described.

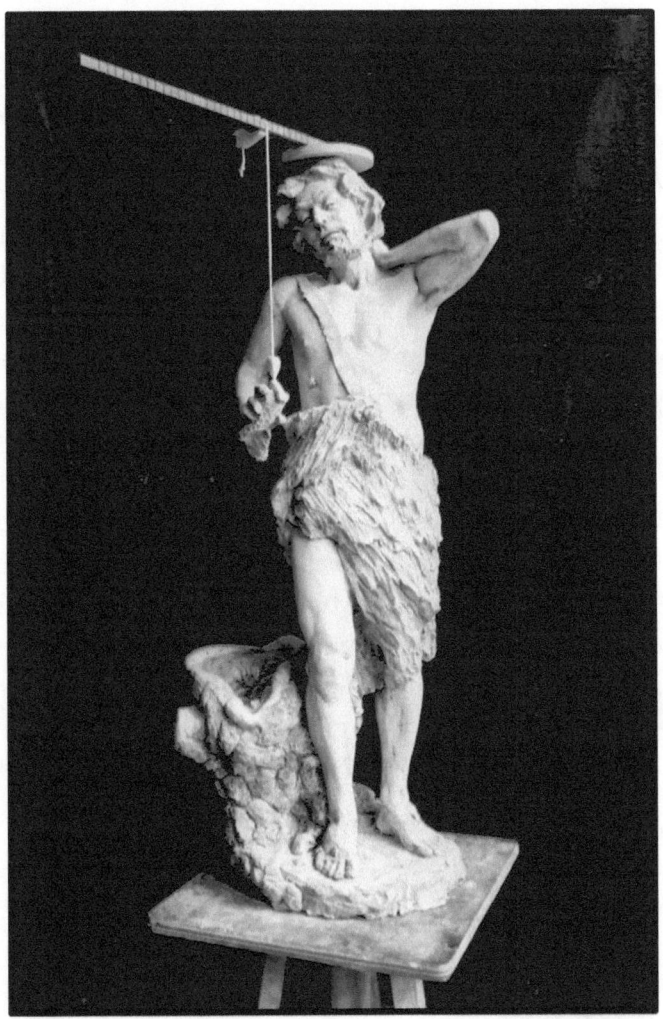

7. For the purposes of demonstration I will use a plaster cast of a sculpture I made. *Wild Honey*, 2011.

---

[6] I do not translate this term for lack of a better word in English.. In Alberti's Latin text it is 'finitorium'. Either have more ring than the English equivalent, "definer".

I make use of this Diffinitore in this way. This applies to the living model, or to a modello from which I want to take the points, say, a statue by Phidias, in which he restrains a chariot horse with his left hand. I set the Diffinitore on top, above the head of the statue, so that it is in every direction level with its center, where I set it with a nail: and I make sure this point above the head of that statue rests at the center of the circle, marking this place with a needle or a pin. Then, I orient the horizon by turning the instrument, so that the degree marked as '1' aligns with the direction of the statue's face. One does it this way: I bring the moving ruler, that is the boom, on which is set the plumbline, to the first degree of the horizon, and thereby stopping at the face; or, I turn the entire circle of the horizon until the thread of the plumbline touches some principal part of the statue, a part more notable than all others, like the finger of the right hand: from here I can move the Diffinitore again and again, how and where I like, and adjust it to as it was when first placed on the statue, that is, so the pin from the top of the statue's head penetrates at the center of Diffinitore, and the plumbline falls from the horizon at the first degree, and hangs to touch that same thumb of his right hand.[7]

---

[7] This paragraph describes the calibration of the device. By aligning the zero point on the horizon with a precise part of the sculpture (a knuckle in the example I show), one can use this to periodically check that the fixed horizon has not moved during the process of setting points; one can also use this measurement to precisely reset the Diffinitore if it should ever be bumped or removed from the statue.

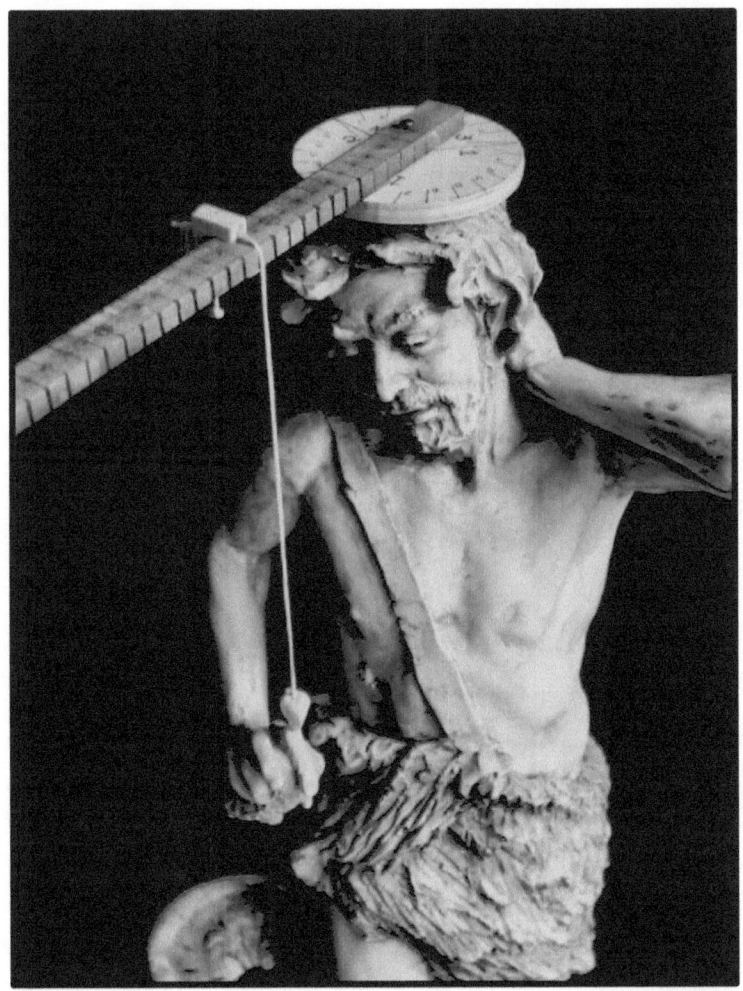

8. With the horizon of the Diffinitore set at '1', a plumbline touches the knuckle of the statue's hand. Should the Diffinitore ever be removed from the statue, this measurement can be used to reposition and recalibrate it.

These things positioned and controlled, I may now truly take the measurement of the angle of the left elbow, and memorize it, and even write it down - I do it this way: I fix this Diffinitore, the instrument being with its center at the top of the head of the statue, in the aforementioned place and state, so that the horizon is quite firm and immovable, and turn the boom until the plumbline touches the left elbow of the statue that we wanted to study.

In doing things this way, we need three things to achieve our purpose. First, we take note of the boom's movement on the horizon from that place from whence we first placed it, paying attention to what minute on the horizon the boom strikes, the twentieth, or thirtieth, or any other; Secondly, take note of the inches and minutes marked upon the boom, which is how much the elbow protrudes from the center of the horizon; and third, finally, we note how many inches and how many minutes the elbow is found from the floor, by placing the ruler on the ground level of the statue. And write these measurements in your notebook in this way: the angle of the left elbow on the horizon is at 10 degrees, 5 minutes; on the boom 7 degrees, 3 minutes; and from the floor on the ruler 40 degrees, 4 minutes.[8]

And so, with this same method you will take note of all the other most notable parts of the statue, or living model, how and where you find them, as for example, the points of the knees, and shoulders, and other projections. But if you want to measure the hollows and concavities, when they are to be found where the plumbline cannot reach, as occurs in the concavity below the shoulders at the kidneys, you can conveniently mark it in this way: attach to the boom another plumb line that falls to this concavity, at whatever distance you like from the first plumbline, it does not matter: for through these two plumblines, you end up with a plane, hanging as they do from a straight surface above, which intersects both of these lines in a row and penetrates into the center of the statue. You can measure from the second plumbline towards the center of the Diffinitore, which is called the center axis.

---

[8] This describes triangulation; these measurements lie on the three spatial axes in relation to the zero point (the center of the horizon). All pointing systems use triangulation. See the commentary for more on this.

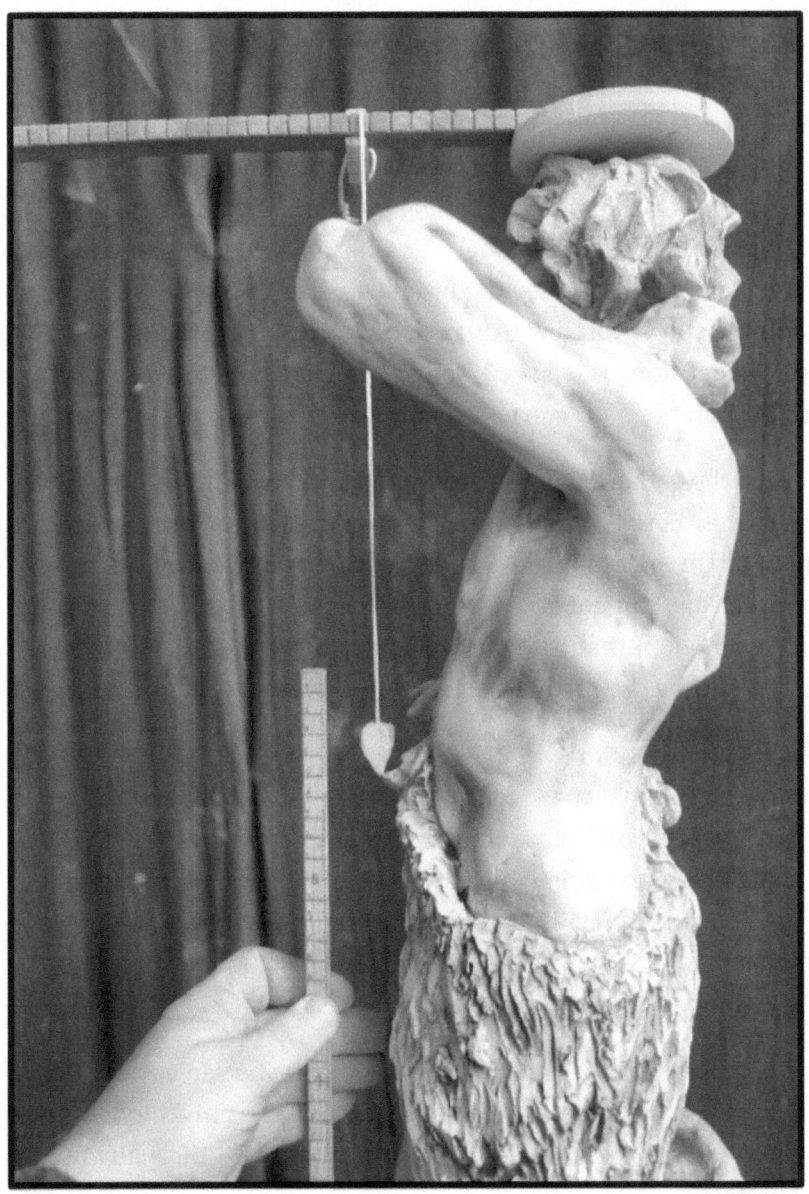

9. Taking a point on a sculpture using three measurements: the radial marking on the horizon, length along the boom, and elevation from the floor.

On Sculpture

If you understand these things sufficiently, you will easily imagine that which I mentioned previously: namely, that if a statue has been covered up with a thickness of wax or clay, you can pierce it quickly, reliably and easily, arriving at any point or feature known on the statue. It is evident that with the turn of the boom, you move the plumbline in such a way that it draws a curved line in the shape of the surface of a column surrounding this statue. If this is so, then with the same method of penetrating the air with the ruler you can arrive at a point - let us say the prominence of the chin - while the statue was not covered with wax or clay; the same principle will apply, penetrating the wax or clay as you would the air, taking into account that the air is converted into wax or clay.

Through these things I have recounted, you can comfortably do what I mentioned before, that is, make half your statue in Carrara, and the other half on the island of Paros. If I saw my modello by Phidias into two parts, and this cut is done on a flat plane - let us say at the waist - I have no doubt that with the aid of our Diffinitore, I can locate as many points as I want, and we can record points circling around the edge of the cut.

If you grant me that these things are possible, you can undoubtedly record any part you like. Seeing this, you can mark on the modello a little red line at the point you will make the horizontal cut, if the statue was cut, and with the points marked along this, you are given the opportunity to finish the job. Still other things can be done, as I have explained.

Finally, through all the things I have said here, you see very plainly that you can take the measurements and points from a modello, or live figure quite conveniently, to make a work of art through reason and perfect craftsmanship.

Commentary - On the Setting of Points.

Set points give us the momentary variety of limbs caused by various poses, and movements of the parts, and teaches us placement and location.

In this section, Alberti describes a tool and a technique for transferring any given point off the surface of a three-dimensional object, to be used to develop a copy of that object. The family of tools to which Alberti's belongs is that of pointing machines. The geometric principle behind this technique is called triangulation[9].

Pointing machines are very much still in use today, taking various forms. Alberti's is one of the earliest, if not the earliest, described. (The ancient Greeks and Romans had their measuring systems as well, but descriptions of their exact methods and devices used are scant.) Alberti's is also the most unwieldy and least utilized design; however, the principles upon which it is based are fundamental to all devices that have since followed.

Alberti's Diffinitore works by measuring several distances, angles, and radii to come up with a three-dimensional relationship between two points; these points are the 'zero point' of the center of the horizon, and the desired point on the surface of the object being measured. Instead of recording the distance between the two as a single linear measurement, as you would with a tape measure or compasses, it is recorded via several geometric inputs – distance

---

[9] More accurately, it's a type of trilateration. Trilateration is a geometric process which provides the same information that triangulation does, but using slightly different inputs. But for now, if you have an idea of what triangulation is about, that's sufficient.

along the length of the boom, degree of the horizon on which the boom lies, and vertical distance from the floor. Thus the point on the surface of the object is described as a combination of three measurements, as Alberti indicates:

And write these measurements in your notebook in this way: the angle of the left elbow on the horizon is at 10 degrees, 5 minutes; on the boom 7 degrees, 3 minutes; and from the floor on the ruler 40 degrees, 4 minutes.

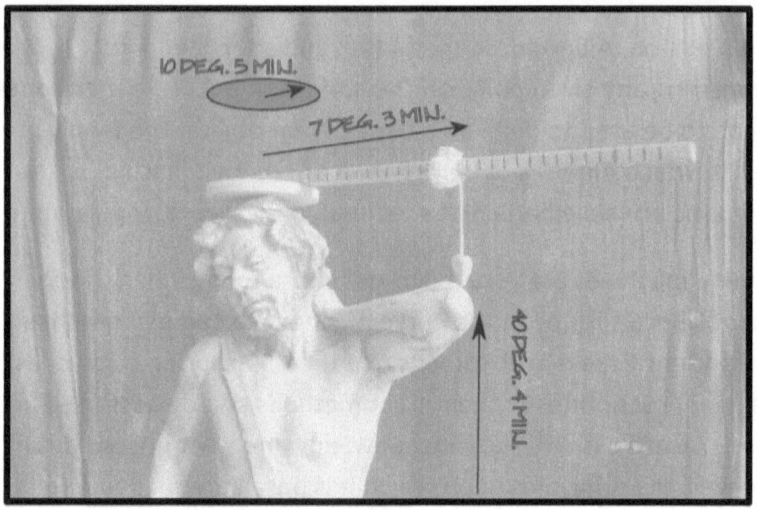

10.

The idea behind using this system of measurement is that it provides a description of the *relation* between these two points in space; linear measurements merely provide the distance between them. In this case, a linear measurement might be from the center of the horizon to the elbow.

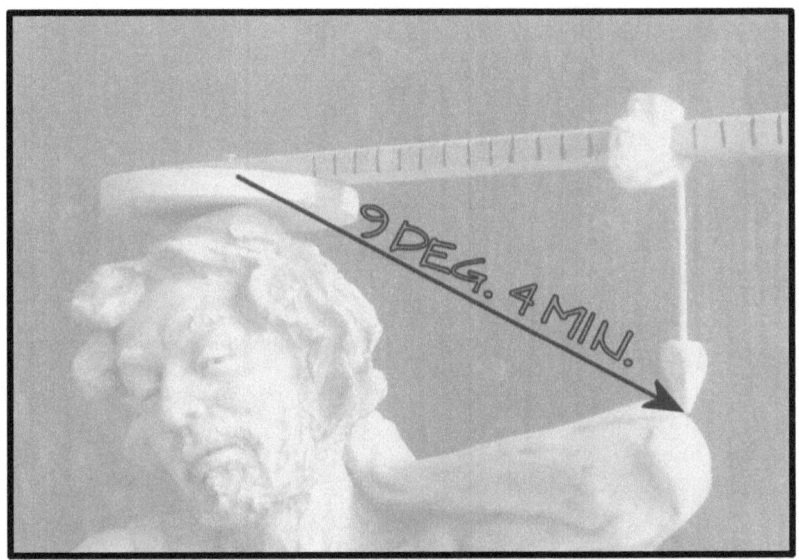

11.

Here's a good analogy of the difference between linear measurement and triangulation: say you wanted to get from your home to the grocery store. Triangulation tells you what streets to take and in what direction to be able to arrive there, while linear measurement only tells you that the store is five miles away, revealing nothing about direction.

Another example of a pointing device utilizing triangulation is the 'chassis' system, seen illustrated in Eduard Lanteri's <u>Modelling</u>.

Two wooden frames (or chassis), one reduced in proportion to the other, are built around the original and around the armature for the clay enlargement. The arms of the frames are marked off with proportionate units, just like the two rulers are made according to Albert's instruction for taking dimensions. Using T-squares and plumblines, measurements are taken across the top bar directly above the point desired, up the side bar to the height of the point, and then using a ruler perpendicular to the arms of the frame, a measurement is taken into the frame itself to touch the original at

41

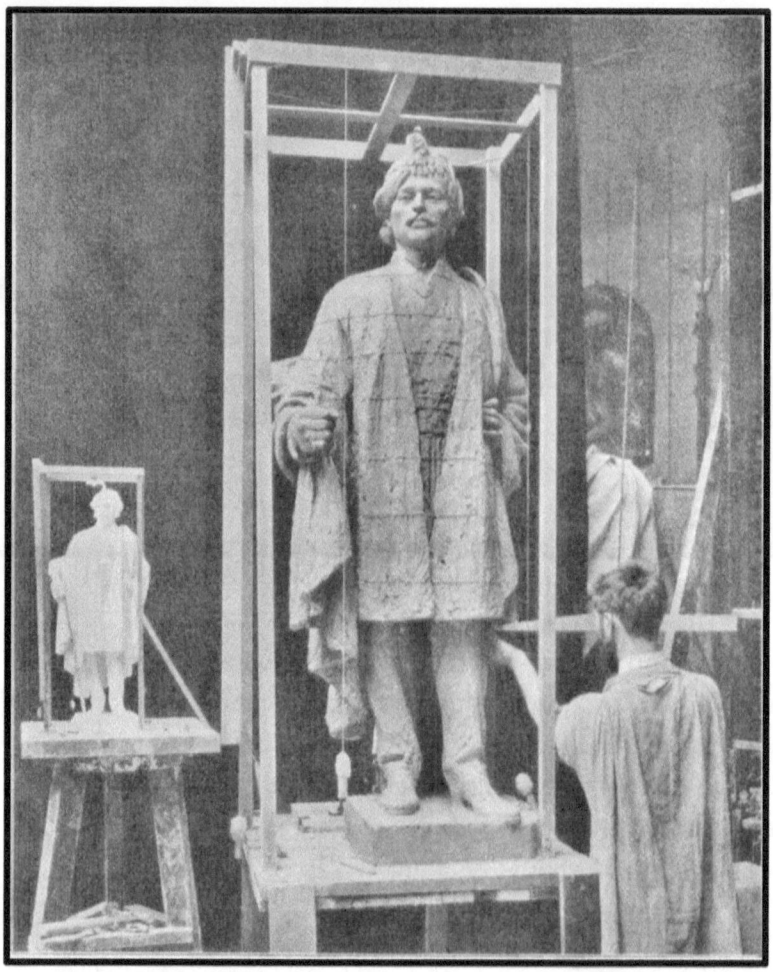

12. The Chassis System, as described by Eduard Lanteri in Modeling, Vol. III (now republished as Modeling and Sculpting Animals, Dover Press).

the point desired. The proportional difference between the frames determines scale of enlargement or reduction of the figure. Lanteri also illustrates a similar system for pointing up a relief.

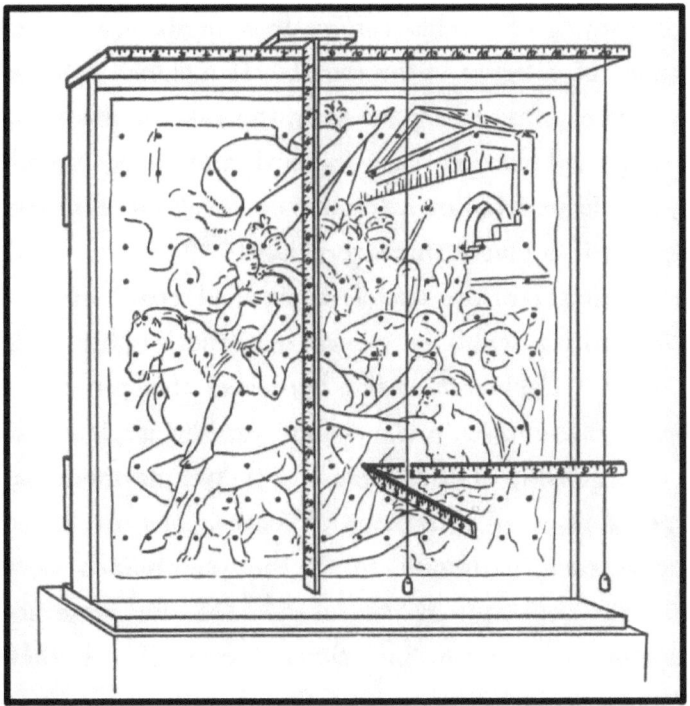

13. From Lanteri's <u>Modeling</u>, showing a relief being pointed up.

The pointing device in most common use today is called in Italian *macchinetta per punti*, often abbreviated to *macchinetta*, or known simply as the pointing machine, and its design is ingenious. Instead of locating each point along three axes, as in the chassis system, or from a zero point, as in Alberti's Diffinitore, the pointing machine fixes a point in space relative to three other known points – first on the modello, and then in the marble, or whatever material into which you are copying the modello.

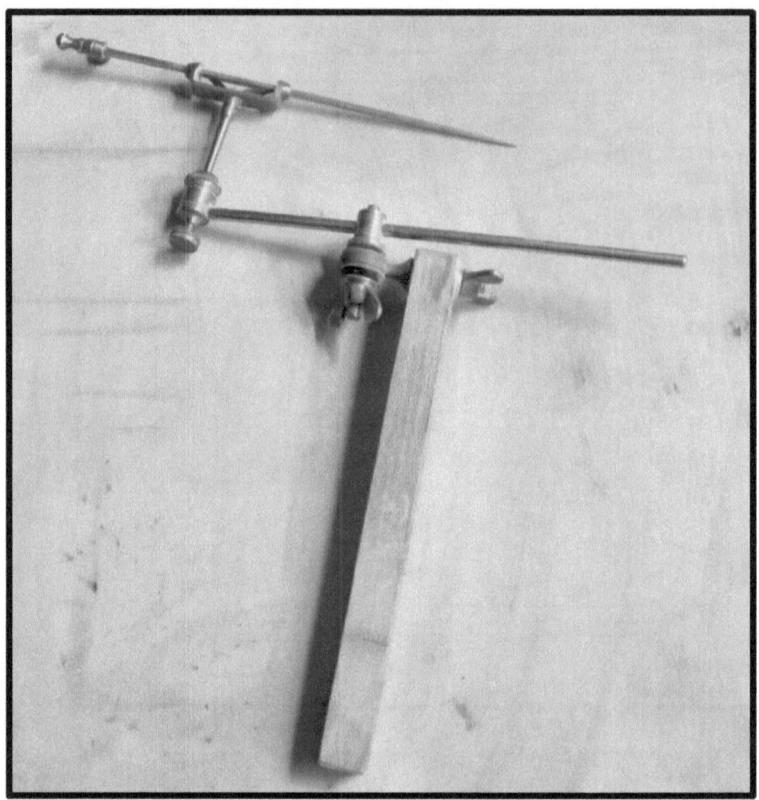

14. The macchinetta, shown here removed from its crossbar tripod, which is called a *croce (see illustration 15).*

Essentially, the *macchinetta* is a tripod, supporting a jointed and adjustable arm. Its three legs are fixed and immobile, relative to each other. These legs taper into something like the point of a nail. These in turn sit on three nailheads set into the plaster cast, as shown in illustration 15), and also into three small holes drilled into the marble. This tripod, called a *croce* or crosswood, thus has a fixed position both on the original and on the copy. You can take it off and put it back onto the work a hundred times, and it will always sit in the same way.

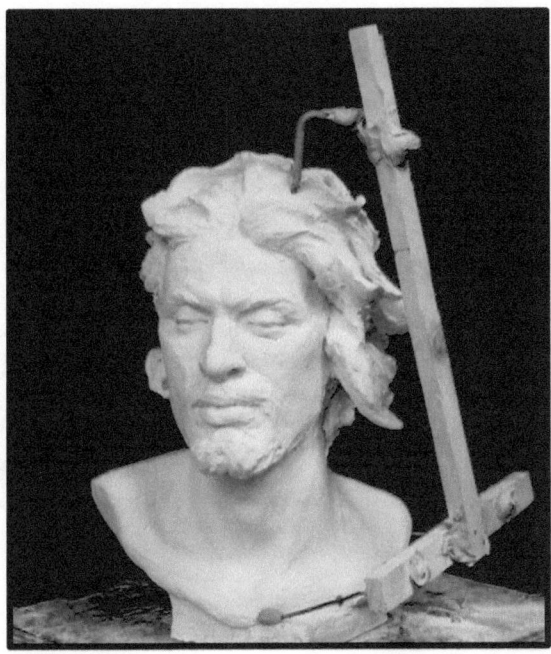

15. The croce, sitting on three nailheads driven into a model of a bust. Small holes have been drilled into the nailheads so the points of the croce's 'feet' sit snugly, and in exactly the same manner, every time the croce is removed and replaced. Three identical holes will be drilled into the marble block; and the croce, macchinetta attached, moves from one to the other.

How the pointing machine takes measurements is by the user locking down the adjustable arm so that the tip of the needle mounted into the arm touches the point on the surface of the plaster cast; then, the pointing machine is lifted off the cast, placed into its position on the copy in progress, where the needle now indicates the position of that point below the surface of the marble. The needle will strike the surface of the marble at the location where the sculptor will need to carve in to find that final point. If the copy is to be in clay, the needle will indicate a point in empty space, to which the sculptor will then add clay until the volume of the work reaches the point indicated.

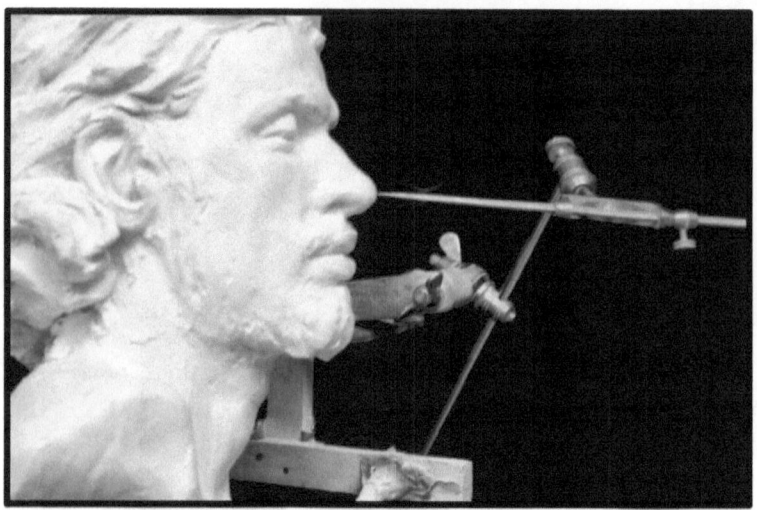

16. The macchinetta, now attached to the croce, is adjusted to touch a small pencil dot made on the tip of the nose.

The pointing machine eliminates the need for bulky frames or for unwieldy boom arms and plumblines; but most importantly, it almost completely eliminates the possibility of miscalibration. Miscalibration happens when, for instance, one of your frames for the chassis system is accidentally bumped and thereby moved relative to the original or the copy. Or, in the case of Alberti's Diffinitore, the device is bumped so that the horizon is no longer perfectly level, or is rotated away from its zero mark, as mentioned in the footnotes of section 4.

Having been developed in the late eighteenth century, the pointing machine is a relatively new triangulation device. In contemporary times we have seen the use of the pointing machine slowly give way to computerized devices which create a digital three-dimensional scan of the original, combined with routing machines that cut the copy into stone or 3D printers which replicate the original in plastics, resins, and a variety of other materials. Every device along this evolution has had the Diffinitore as its common ancestor,

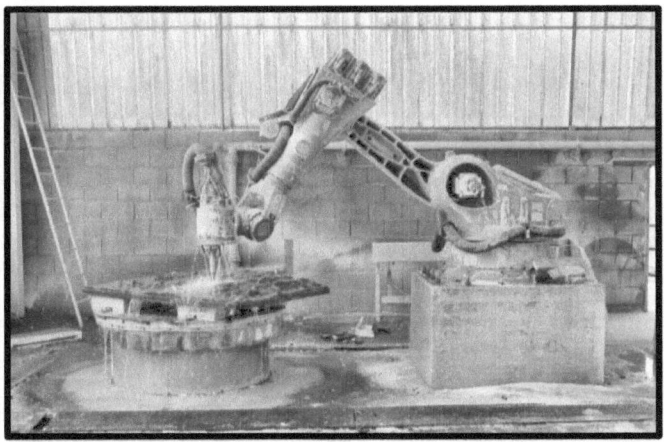

17. Robotic arm cutting a relief in dark marble. Water is used to cool the cutting head and to wash away marble dust.

Triangulation did not commence with the Diffinitore, however. These pointing devices are really nothing more than conveniences for quickly and accurately measuring what we can also measure using linear measuring tools, like rulers and compasses. Triangulation with compasses is perhaps the grandfather of pointing methods. This method does not employ a device that can be knocked out of calibration, requiring nothing more than several sets of compasses, which are easy enough to come by. Compasses are also useful in the sculptor's studio in many other applications, and so chances are sculptors own a few of these tools even if they have never pointed up a figure with them.

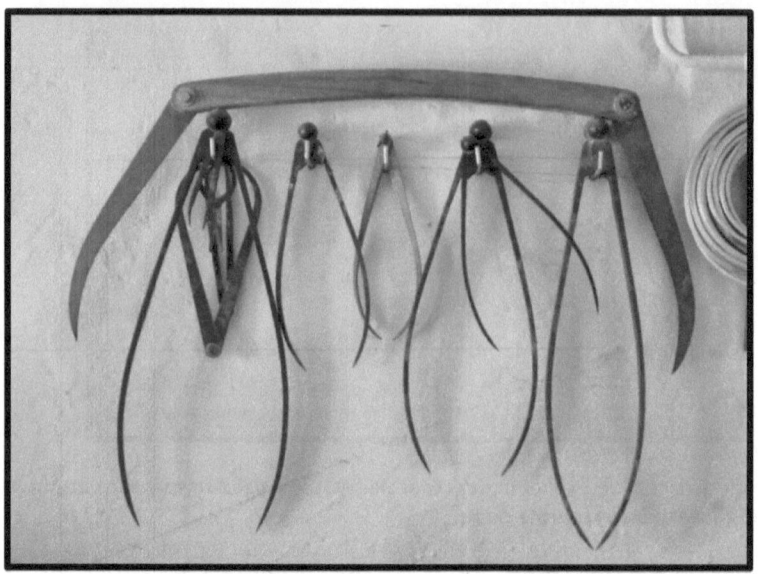

18. A set of sculptor's compasses.

There is a very widespread misunderstanding about the proper use of compasses, as I mentioned earlier. It is common to find sculptors who take linear measurements (point A to point B) with compasses across the surface of their living model or plaster cast, and apply that measurement directly to their work, in order to build up a figure. This is incorrect usage. Linear measurements can *only* give the distance between two points, but give nothing in terms of their relationship in three dimensional space. This is something only triangulation can do. Thus we can measure the distance between the corners of a mouth, for instance, but that distance tells us nothing about how deeply set into the face these points are, the elevations of these points relative to each other, or how both points relate to the rest of the face and the volume of the head. This confounds the beginner, who can't get over how wrong the mouth looks even though "the measurement says it is right". Better not to use them than to use them incorrectly.

To triangulate with compasses correctly, one simply finds the distance of each point from three other known points. These known points, sometimes called *capopunti* or 'head points', are usually located in the base of the plaster cast from which you are copying. You determine the locations of capopunti similar to the way you find a point via the chassis system – measuring up from the bottom, across the side or front, and then towards the center. Then locate three points on the base of your marble with a relation between them identical to the first set on the plaster cast. Once you are certain of the congruous relationship of one set of points to the other, you can measure from each of these points on the model and apply the results to the modello.

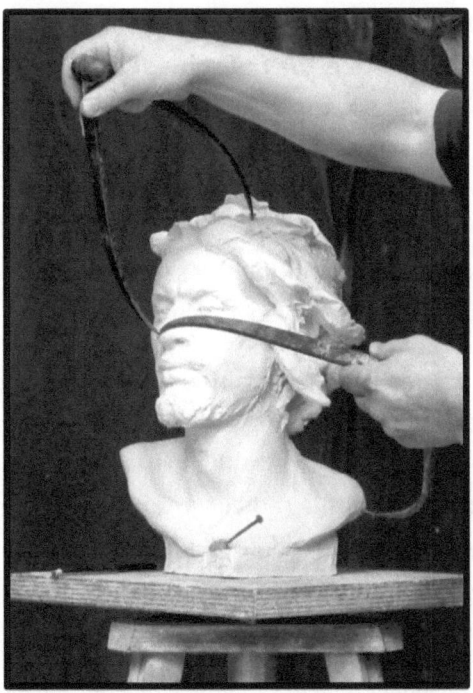

19. Using compasses to measure to the nose from two 'known' points - the capopunti. When the measurement from the third capopunto is taken, I will have three measurements which describe the position of the tip of the nose, similar to the three measurements taken with the Diffinitore.

On Sculpture

This method has been used by sculptors for hundreds of years, but probably not as far back as Alberti's day. Though triangulation with compasses sounds simple enough, it is a tricky and tedious process and requires practice. It's little wonder, then, that Alberti endeavored to design a device for sculptors to aid them in this practice. But how successful was his Diffinitore?

The lack of evidence that such a device was ever built by Alberti or by other sculptors of his generation should tell us something. We can easily imagine questions arising in the minds of sculptors before ever attempting to construct one, questions Alberti does not address. How is the Diffinitore to be mounted upon the head of a living model? Is a separate Diffinitore to be made for the modello, or is there just one that is transferred back and forth like the *macchinetta*? Then there is the question of keeping the device calibrated – no small task, for if the horizon is even the least bit out of dead level, the smallest discrepancy is magnified by the boom into enormous error. My guess is that throughout the years sculptors recognized the value of the device in theory, and fashioned their own, more practical devices along the same principles when needed... but with at least one spectacular exception.

Gutzon Borglum, the European-trained American sculptor of the Mount Rushmore Monument in South Dakota, devised an enormous Diffinitore to carve the sixty-foot tall faces of four U.S. presidents into granite. Complete with a radial center, boom arm, and a plumbline, Borglum transferred points from a small scale model surmounted by a scaled-down Diffinitore. Thus Alberti's assertion-

Through these means and aids, you will not create anything other than a likeness to it - or a smaller one, or ultimately one of such greatness, even of a hundred fathoms; do not doubt, I desire to say, that you could not make one as big as Mount Caucasus, as long as these grand undertakings do not lack the means.

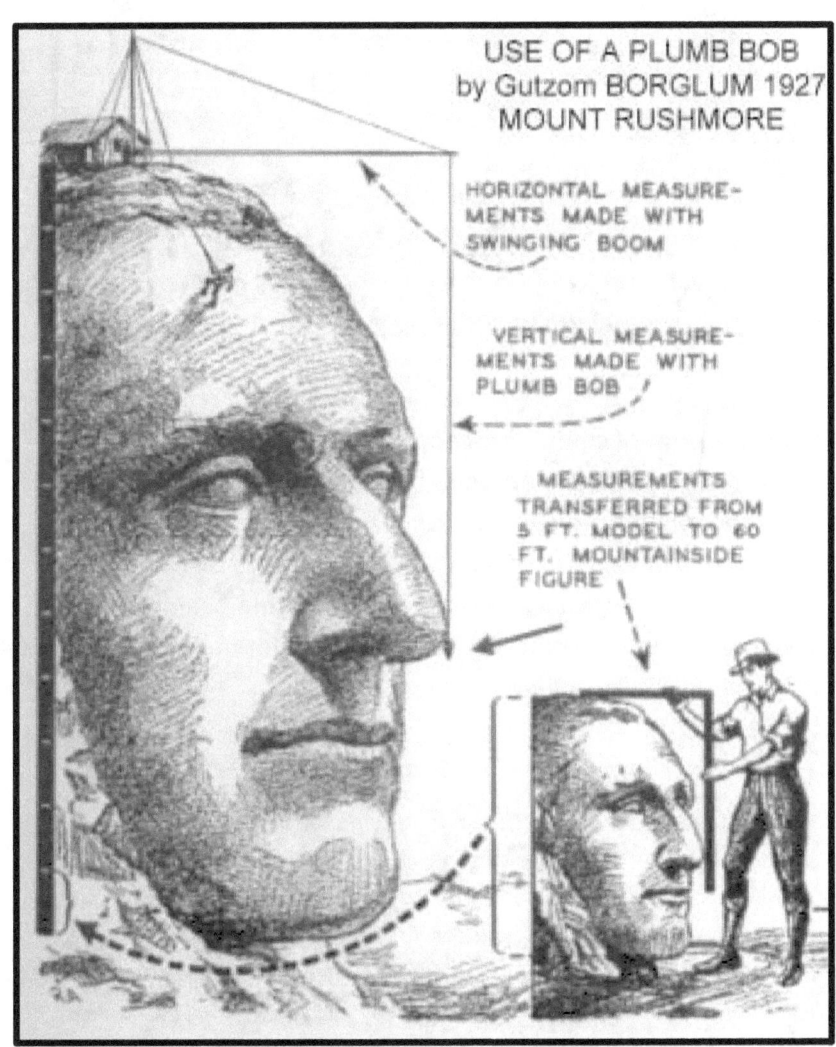

USE OF A PLUMB BOB
by Gutzom BORGLUM 1927
MOUNT RUSHMORE

HORIZONTAL MEASURE-
MENTS MADE WITH
SWINGING BOOM

VERTICAL MEASURE-
MENTS MADE WITH
PLUMB BOB

MEASUREMENTS
TRANSFERRED FROM
5 FT. MODEL TO 60
FT. MOUNTAINSIDE
FIGURE

20. From an article in Modern Mechanix Magazine, 1933

-was more prophesy than fantasy.

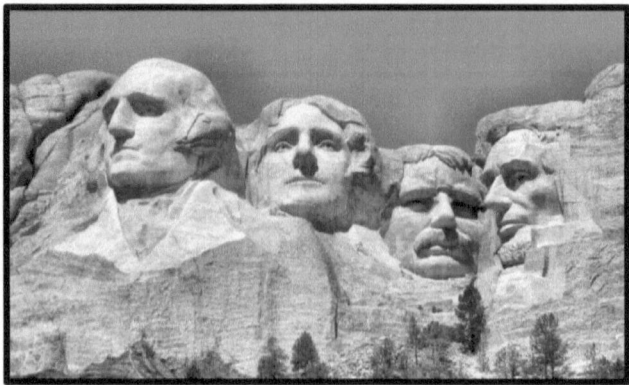

21

Until the advent of computer scanning, the compass system remained the standard method for enlarging and reducing, while use of the *macchinetta* provided for full scale copying. Because of the living model's inability to remain absolutely still, or to return to precisely the same pose each and every time from beginning of the work until the end, no pointing devices have ever been in common use for modelling from life.

...But if you want to measure the hollows and concavities, when they are to be found where the plumbline cannot reach, ... attach to the boom another plumb line, that falls to this concavity, at whatever distance you like from the first plumbline, it does not matter: for through these two plumblines, you end up with a plane, hanging as they do from a straight surface above, which intersects both of these lines in a row, and penetrates into the center of the statue. You can measure from the second plumbline towards the center of the Diffinitore, which is called the center axis.

The idea of measuring with the ruler from a plumbline on the boom to a concave surface on the figure is simple enough. But Alberti's process for measuring points located in the concavities of a figure requires clarification. Dropping a second plumbline from the boom gives the sculptor two lines that lie on the same vertical plane. Because they are hanging off the boom, which originates at the center of the horizon, the vertical plane upon which they both lie intersects an imaginary axis running down from the horizon's center.

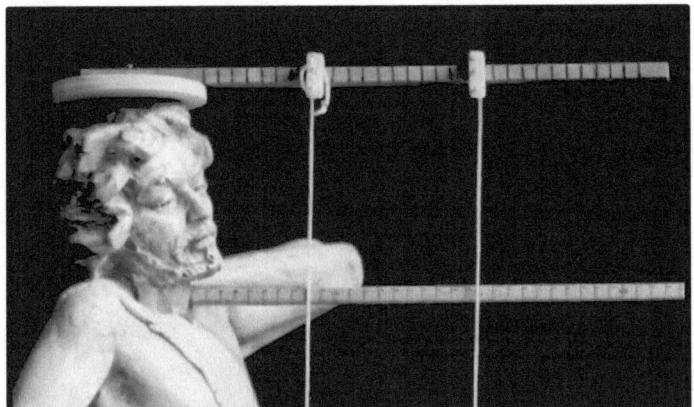

22. Using the ruler to locate a point in a hollow. Subtract the distance on the ruler from the distance on the boom. The second plumbline acts as a guide so that the ruler is held parallel with the boom. If the ruler is not parallel, the measurement will be inaccurate.

Using two plumblines and measuring from the external line, so that the ruler touches both lines and thus lies on this vertical plane, ensures that the ruler is running parallel to the boom pointed directly towards the center axis of the figure. Without two lines as a guide, it is very easy to hold the ruler a little off from being parallel to the boom, which would then give an inaccurate reading.

This method of alignment is also a very old practice, used by astronomers, land surveyors, cartographers, navigators and architects. What you achieve with the alignment of two objects is a *bearing*. Usually, though, instead of using a straight ruler, one uses the line of sight along two objects in alignment to find a bearing. The object nearest the eye is known as the backsight, and the other is the foresight. Gunsights and orienteering compass sights are examples of these.

For a more detailed discussion of the use of optics in sculpture, refer to the commentary of Section 6.

5. On the Measurements of Man.

I wish that this way of working to be familiar with my picture-makers and sculptors, which if the heed me, they will rejoice in it. And because it is through clear examples that I may endeavor to aid the greatest number, I have taken the trouble to describe the main measurements that are in Man. And not merely the details of this or of that man; but as far as I could, I wanted to fix that precise beauty, granted as a gift from Nature, the nearly universal specified proportions given to many bodies - and even put it in writing , in imitation of the man from Croton who in making the statue of a goddess, went around choosing from several virgins, beautiful above all other women, the finest and rarest and most endowed particulars of beauty that is seen in youth, and then put it in his statue.

In this same way I have chosen many bodies, each healthy and beautiful, and I extracted all of their measurements and proportions; then I made comparisons, laying aside the excesses of the extreme, if any were exaggerated or larger than others, and retrieved the median from several bodies and models, which I am calling the most laudatory. After measuring these most notable lengths and widths and thicknesses, I found that my work is complete.

That said, the lengths of the parts are[10]:

Elevation from the ground	Feet	Deg.	Min.
Dorsum of the foot	0	3	0
Outer ankle	0	2	2
Inner ankle	0	3	1
Bottom of medial gastrocnemius	0	8	5
Bottom of interior tibial crest	1	4	3
Bottom of the vastus lateralis	1	7	0
Bottom of testicles, line of buttocks	2	6	9
Pubic symphysis	3	0	0
Great trochanter	3	1	1
Navel	3	6	0
Waist (height of last rib?)	3	7	9

---

[10] The Latin edition of Della Statua ('De Statua') which appeared around the same time as the Italian text contains the additional measurements:

Heights from the ground:

Lower point of the shoulder blades	4	2	5
Top of head from the chin	0	8	0
Ear to chin	0	3	0

Widths:

Width of pelvis above hips	1	0	0
Width of waist (Below ribcage?)	0	9	0
Distance between nipples	0	7	0
Width of neck	0	3	5

Thicknesses (from front to back):

From chest to back	0	7	5
Throat to seventh cervical vertebrae	0	4	0
Forehead to back of head	0	6	4
Thickness of deltoid	0	3	0

On Sculpture

Nipples and bottom of sternum	4	3	5
Suprasternal notch	5	0	0
7th cervical vertebrae (nape of neck)	5	1	0
Chin	5	2	0
Ear	5	5	0
Hairline at the forehead	5	9	0
Middle finger of the hand	2	3	0
Wrist	3	0	0
Elbow	3	8	5
Trapezius at highest point	5	1	8

Lateral Widths	Feet	deg.	Min.
Max. Width of foot	0	4	2
Heel	0	2	3
Ankles	0	2	4
Foreleg above ankles	0	1	5
Below Gastrocnemius	0	2	5
Max. Width of Gastrocnemius	0	3	5
Below Tibial crest	0	3	5
Condyles of the Femur	0	4	0
Thigh at the hollow above knee	0	3	5
Midpoint of thigh	0	5	5

Top of thigh	1	1	1
Chest at armpits	1	1	5
Shoulders	1	5	0
Zygomatic bones of the cranium	0	4	8

The thickness and width of the arms vary according to use, but generally they are as follows:

	Feet	Deg.	Min.
Wrist	0	2	3
Elbow and biceps	0	3	2
Top of arm below Deltoideus	0	4	0

Thickness, from anterior to posterior	Feet	Deg.	Min.
Big toe to heel	1	0	0
Below ankles at Achilles' Tendon	0	4	3
Foreleg above ankles	0	3	0
Foreleg at bottom of Gastrocnemius	0	3	6
Max thickness of Gastrocnemius	0	4	0
Knee at patella	0	4	0
Max thickness of thigh	0	6	0
Torso at pubis	0	7	5
Torso at navel	0	7	0
Torso at waist (below last rib?)	0	6	6

By these means, you can easily take into account the proportions of each limb in comparison with the entire length of the body, and the proportions and correlations they may have within themselves and with one another, and how they vary, or are different. I judge that you should know this, as it a very useful science.

Commentary - On the Measurements of Man.

In this short section, Alberti lays out a canon of proportions derived from the averages of measurements taken from a group of men Alberti himself found to be the most aesthetically pleasing. This relates directly with one of Alberti's two paths towards sculpting a likeness, discussed in Section 2. Working from a canon of proportions is the natural extension of the method of sculpting by 'Dimensions', the method Alberti describes as leading towards a general or an ideal figure.

When utilized for the purposes described by Alberti, a canon of proportions can be a helpful tool. A canon can be applied in painting; for instance, when a figure of a particular person is represented several times in several paintings, such as a fresco cycle on the wall of a church, or a character in a comic book. The proportions of Superman should not change in stature from one panel to the next, and so reliance on a canon to ensure similarity from one rendering to the next makes a lot of sense.

A canon can also be used as a tool for an artist to understand his own aesthetic. Alberti's selection of men he found visually pleasing was naturally subjective, and therefore should not be taken as any sort of law of beauty; but this subjectivity gives us an understanding of Alberti's personal taste. It might be an illuminating exercise if every artist followed Alberti's example, if for no other reason than to understand one's own ideal in representing the figure.

Alberti's method of measuring several examples and devising an average is one method of creating a canon; we might call this an *anthropometric* canon. Another system, that of a *comparative* canon, is one which seeks to establish relations in proportion between different parts of the body. In a comparative canon, the proportions of the body are thought to have a common denominator, to be found within the dimensions of a single body feature. For example: Taking the width of a finger at its root, we can say the palm is four fingers wide; a foot is four palms long, a man is twenty-four palms high, etc. etc. Another example is to imagine the body as eight heads high: the distance from elbow to tip of fingers is two heads, the height of the pelvis is one head, the width of the hips is one and a half heads, etc. Heads, eyes, fingers, palms, feet, and noses have all been used as common denominators for the dimensions of the human body, in various canons.

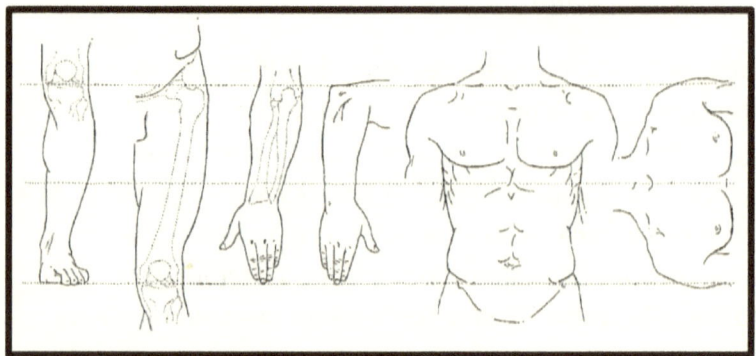

23. From Paul Richer's Anatomie Artistique. A comparative canon, which gives the length of the distance from knee to foot as equal to the upper leg, lower arm, upper arm, height of torso, and width of shoulders.

A comparative canon seeks to emphasize geometric relationships contained within the human form. If Alberti's canon is a personal language of aesthetic preferences, comparative canons are more formal, based as they are on mathematical relationships imposed upon the body, instead of observed relationships.

Of course, neither anthropometric nor comparative canons correspond exactly with any individual subject – but individuality is not the goal when using a canon. Its usefulness or uselessness depends upon each artist's intention. If an artist seeks to understand their own preferences and wishes to consciously work within their own sense of aesthetics, a personal study and creation of an anthropometric canon may be desirable. If an artist does not have ready access to models or does not know how to properly work from living subjects, comparative canons may serve the purpose. Comparative canons may also be helpful in emulating the aesthetics of Classical Greek statuary, or other historical styles.

Many canons have been devised and have proliferated in studios and in schools for so long, that many beginner students - and even teachers - take certain easy comparisons as truths. These shortcuts are dangerous especially where the topic of portraiture is concerned. The myth of the 'five-eye head' – the width of the head being five 'eyes' wide – or of the vertical division of the face into thirds corresponding with major facial features are antithetical to the very nature of portraiture, which demands individual observation. (It is my opinion that some sculptors cling to this shorthand out of an ignorance of methods of optical observation of the living model. These sculptors seek out a standard method of creating a recognizably human head, upon which they then adorn superficial features characteristic of their subject. Thus the state of contemporary portrait sculpture.)

For an excellent and concise survey of various canons of proportion, I recommend Dr. Paul Richer's Artistic Anatomy, translated into English by Robert Beverly Hale. In addition to being a fundamental text on human anatomy for the artist, there is a short chapter on canons from various periods in art history from the Egyptians to the École des Beaux-Arts in the nineteenth century (but omitting the work of Alberti, which may well have been unknown to the author), and includes a comparative canon designed by the Richer himself, who was both medical surgeon and sculptor.

On Sculpture

Speaking of artistic anatomy, one cannot overestimate the importance, when working with canons, of a thorough grasp of anatomy. No canon can be complete enough to describe through simple measurements the interconnectivity of musculature and bones that comprise a figure. The measurements are merely anchors upon which a figure is tethered- it is not the figure itself. Anatomical knowledge at least is needed, but more preferable still is knowledgeable use of the live model.

As for Alberti's canon in particular, I was curious to see what sort of figure it would lead to, and so took it upon myself to model a clay sketch of a figure using these proportions. I did not use a live model, but merely generalized the main anatomical points and modeled the figure in the 'anatomical position' of a standing figure with supine arms, so as not to cloud the visibility of the given proportions.

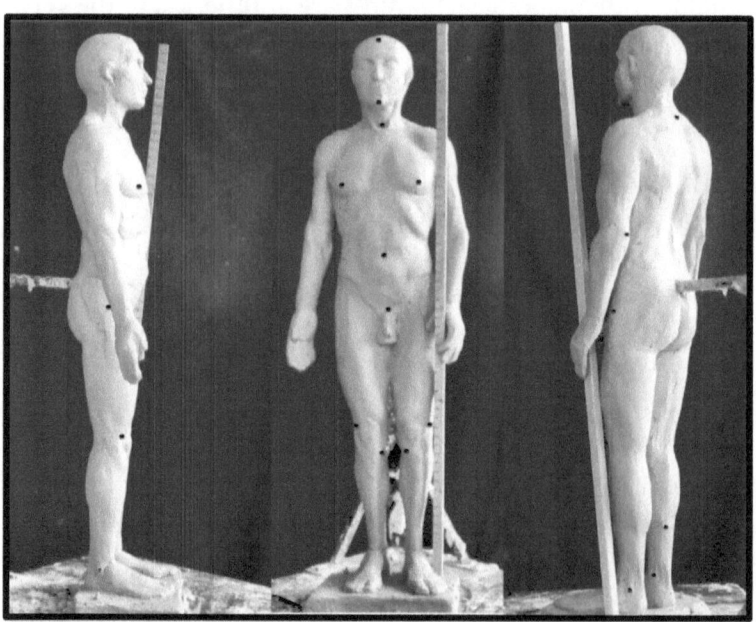

24. Alberti's Measurements of Man applied to a clay sketch. The figure holds the ruler with which the figure's proportions were calculated. The black dots on the figure represent points from which the figure was measured.

To me, the proportions appear somewhat ungraceful; the pit of the throat is too high, making the neck appear short. The measurements given for the width of the thighs contrast so much with the thin forelegs, I wonder whether there was an error made in the recording of either measurement. The width of the foot is given as almost three times that of the width of the foreleg above the ankles, which seems extreme. I wonder if Alberti's ideal foreleg was ever found in the same living subject as Alberti's ideal foot.

As in all canons, these measurements are meant to serve as a rough guide, which the artist will vary according to his taste. Whatever its faults, Alberti's canon has the virtue of being the product of personal taste, observation, and analysis, rather than an arbitrary comparative shorthand.

6. On further topics of study.

I could tell you of many things; that which changes in a man when he is seated or standing, or leaning towards this or to that side. But I leave these things to the diligence and the fastidiousness of those who are doing the work. Also beneficial is the knowledge of the number of bones and muscles, and their projections.

And besides this, it is greatly useful to know the rule by which we separate circumferences, and divide bodies by the views of the parts that cannot be seen; for example, as if someone cut in half an upright cylinder, so that the part which presents itself to the eye was divided and removed from that part out of view. Such a cylinder would be made into two bodies, in which the base of one would be in all respects similar to the base of another, and would have the same shape, being comprised of the same four lines and circles. This is similar to the observation of the sections of bodies, so called; seeing as how the contour of that line, which separates what you see of the figure from what you do not see, should operate in a similar fashion.

And truly this outline, were you to draw it on a wall, observing the wall in the same way, there would be represented a figure very similar to a shadow that was projected onto it from a light that shone from that same point in the air in which one had found the eye of the observer. But this method of drawing things by means of observation of contours and sections pertains more to the Painter than the Sculptor, and I will discuss it at another time. Further, those who wish to make this art their profession should know principally the distance of every projection or hollow of any member from a particular disposition of lines.

Commentary - On further topics of study.

This final, hasty section is both tantalizing and frustrating. Alberti gives the reader a short list of what he would explain about the art of sculpture, if he had the time...

I could tell you of many things...

...giving the entire treatise an unfinished air. Some scholars contend Alberti tacked on this last section almost by way of an acknowledgement that his work was unfinished. Indeed, Alberti meant to flesh out his ideas about the visual study of objects in a more comprehensive work; intending to discuss it, as he says, "at another time." A more complete understanding of Alberti's thoughts on the practice of sculpture needs to include other relevant passages found elsewhere in his bibliography. Chiefly, this is to be found in Alberti's treatise known in English as On Painting.

In the past, publishers and translators have resolved this issue by bundling Della Statua with Della Pittura (On Painting's title in Italian; also historically available in Latin as De Pictura) in the same volume. While Della Pittura is indeed the source for further insight for the sculptor, no mention is ever made in these editions concerning which sections of Della Pittura have anything to do with sculpture or Alberti's "further topics". Much of Della Pittura raises issues relevant solely to the painter, and to my knowledge no editor has bothered to sift through the work and pick out those points relevant to both painting and sculpture in the first text which more fully completes the second.

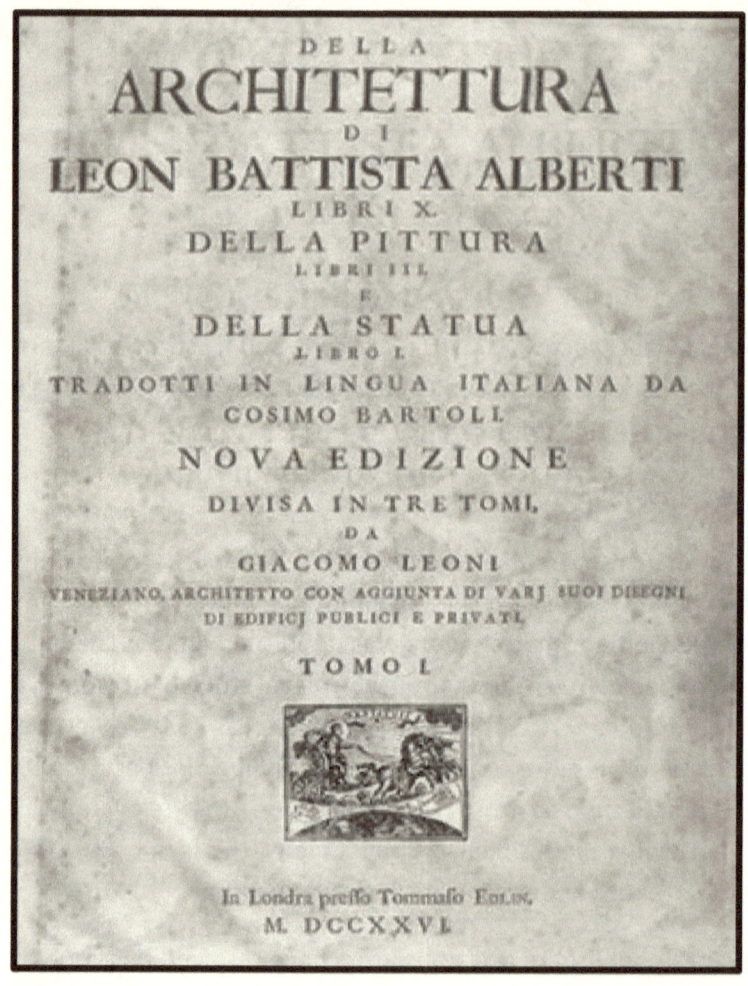

25. One of the many editions over the centuries that bundles <u>On Sculpture</u> with <u>On Painting</u>.

Before I do so, let's return to the final section of <u>Della Statua</u> to understand what specifically we are looking for in Alberti's writing elsewhere. After a brief mention of the importance of studying anatomy, and of studying the live model in various poses to determine alterations to the standard canon of proportions, Alberti struggles to explain the concept of studying a figure's contour – as he puts it,

...the rule by which we separate circumferences, and divide bodies by the views of the part that cannot be seen...

Alberti tries to make us understand what he is talking about by examples: that of cutting a cylinder in such a way so that the line of the cut corresponds exactly with the visual boundary of the cylinder from a particular point of view; and that of tracing on a wall the shadow of an object, relating the light source to the observer's viewpoint. We can understand his difficulty to some extent in explaining these optical/sculptural ideas, as Alberti was one of the first to try to do so.

That's not to say that Alberti was one of the first to create a sculpture by observing and replicating the contour of the model – artists have been doing that since sculpture began. But Alberti attempts here to analyze and describe the *process of observation* as applied to the creation of sculpture. It's far easier to discuss measurement, proportion, and anatomical construction of a sculpted figure, as though sculpting a man was like building a house, constructed from plans and blueprints. It's another thing altogether to quantify the act of visual perception, and upon that perception, build a working method.

In the end, Alberti contented himself to direct the reader towards a future explanation:

This method of drawing things by means of observation of contours and sections pertains more to the painter than the sculptor, and I will discuss it at another time.

On Painting – Selected passages

The entire book is well worth knowing for any sculptor. I won't repeat here every tidbit of advice which is to the benefit of sculptors as well as painters, nor all the examples and anecdotes which explain this advice – On Painting is readily available in English from the hands of other publishers and my excessive quotation here would be redundant. Though much relates directly to the practice of sculpture, I confine myself to the subjects Alberti specifically alluded to in the last section in Della Statua . I hope what I point out here will encourage readers to get a hold of a copy of the full text and give it a good and thorough read.

Della Pittura was written in 1435-36, a few decades after the pioneering work by Ghiberti, Donatello, Paolo Uccello, and Brunelleschi had made optical perspective in painting and sculpture popular with artists in Florence. Alberti's contribution was to analyze the practice and describe the science behind it, allowing the techniques of perspective to become more widespread. Alberti made sure to give credit to the artists who pioneered these techniques, even dedicating his treatise to Fillippo Brunelleschi, the genius architect, sculptor, and painter. In his dedication, Alberti even begs Brunelleschi to point out his mistakes, should he find any:

If you find the leisure, it would please me if you should look again at this my little work On Painting which I set into Tuscan for your renown. You will see three books; the first, all mathematics, concerning the roots in nature which are the source of this delightful and most noble art. The second book puts the art in the hand of the artist, distinguishing its parts and demonstrating all. The third introduces the artist to the means and the end, the ability and the desire of acquiring perfect skill and knowledge in painting. May it please you, then, to read me with diligence. If anything here seems to you to need emending, correct me. There was never a writer so learned to whom erudite friends were not useful. I in particular desire to be corrected by you in order not to be pecked at by detractors.[11]

In the three sections of <u>On Painting</u> Alberti mentions, large sections address subjects solely concerning painters – themes and compositions, color, etc. What concerns the sculptor in this work falls into two categories. The 'mathematics' of Book One speak of the geometric relationship between the model (be it a human figure, architecture, or a streetscape), the work of art, and the observer/creator of that work. Parts of Book Two and much of Book Three speak of the studio practice which utilizes this geometric relationship, as well as other general habits and practices of artists.

Alberti's analysis of optics in art recorded in the first section is regarded as his greatest achievement. It is the cornerstone of his treatise <u>Della Pittura</u>, and this treatise disseminated the science of optics and the art of rendering optical perspective to painters all over Europe in the early period of the Florentine Renaissance. He didn't invent perspective – that had been evolving over the previous century, and had been more or less codified by that extraordinary generation of artists which included Ghiberti, Brunelleschi, Donatello, and Pollaiuolo, all of whom can take partial credit for its development. (These artists were themselves standing on the shoulders of mathematical giants, namely Euclid, father of the geometry which bears his name, and Alhazen, the tenth century Persian mathematical genius, whose <u>Book of Optics</u> had been available in Italian and studied by Ghiberti and others.)

The idea of visual perspective is so widespread in our times it seems hardly necessary to explain it here. Even non-artists have learned in

---

[11] This and other excerpts I use are from <u>On Painting, by Leon Battista Alberti,</u> Translated with Introduction and Notes by John R. Spencer. Yale University Press, 1956.

one way or another the basic concepts of the horizon line, the vanishing point, and so on.[12] It is commonly recognized as the body of techniques that give that '3D' effect to two dimensional images.

For an elementary example, here on the left is a two dimensional box, drawn on a picture plane (that is, drawn on this page):

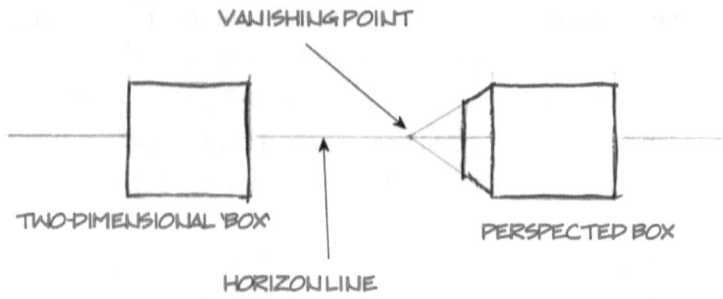

26. The elements of perspective.

Next to it is another box, on the same flat page, but drawn to reveal a side of the box 'receding into the distance', using a vanishing point and a horizon line, giving the illusion of three-dimensional depth.

Book I of <u>Della Pittura</u> is mostly the nuts and bolts of simple plane geometry and one point perspective. Alberti details the definitions of a point, a line, and the various angles and planes; how things appear smaller the farther they are from a certain point of view and other elemental truths; the function of optical 'rays' (lines of sight) that extend in a straight line until they impact upon a surface; and of course, the elements of rendering one point perspective.

But what do the techniques that render the illusion of depth in a painting have to do with sculpture? Apart perhaps from relief work,

---

[12] The meager example of perspective I give here is the tip of the iceberg. For a thorough understanding of one point and three point perspective, you can hardly do better than Rex Vicat Cole's <u>Perspective For Artists</u>, available from Dover Press.

perspective and its methods don't seem to apply to sculpture. Sculpture in the round contains no foreshortening, no concept of a vanishing point, no illusion of 'distance' into which a fully three-dimensional sculpture 'recedes'. Perspective gives the illusion of depth – in sculpture, that depth is real.

The relevance of optical perspective for sculptors begins with the division of the phenomenon of perspective into two separate actions on the part of the artist: *perception* and *rendering*. It is only the *rendering* of perspective that solely concerns painters and not sculptors. *Perception* of perspective, however, is absolutely vital to sculptors who wish to represent anything in nature through sculpture. Perception of perspective, after all, is the visual perception of three-dimensional form.

Let me give an example of the difference between these two facets of perspective. Fillippo Brunelleschi, the painter, sculptor, and architect, was an early experimenter in one point perspective, and may well have been the first to distill it to a mathematical formula. In order to show others how accurately he could render perspective, he set up a demonstration. First, on a wooden panel he painted a scene of the Baptistery, a famous architectural landmark in Florence, using his laws of perspective and a single vanishing point. Then, he invited others to compare his painting to the actual scene. Seems simple enough.

But Brunelleschi was out to prove his accuracy; so rather than merely having people see and recognize the baptistery in his painting, he took his viewers to the very spot where he painted the picture, so they might compare that particular view of the Baptistery with the painting. Still sounds simple? Merely standing on the same spot wasn't precise enough for Brunelleschi, however. What if his viewer was shorter or taller than Brunelleschi, or was standing a little to one side, when making the comparison? That viewer would have a slightly different view of the Baptistery than Brunelleschi did when he painted.

Brunelleschi knew that the only way for others to judge his competence in perspective would be to have them compare his painting to the absolutely specific, single point of view from which the painting was created. Here's how he did that: Brunelleschi drilled a tiny hole though the painting itself, right through the vanishing point. Then, he mounted the painting to an easel so that the tiny hole was at Brunelleschi's own eye height. Viewers were invited to look through the hole from the backside of the painting. What they saw was the Baptistery (the real one, not the painted one); just as Brunelleschi saw it when he painted the picture, but reflected in a mirror he had set up at an angle to the painting. Then, Brunelleschi turned the mirror to face the painting directly. The viewer would now be looking at the painting of the Baptistery, also reflected in the mirror. In this way, Brunelleschi had precise control over the perception of the viewer, who could now compare the painting and the building to each other accurately.

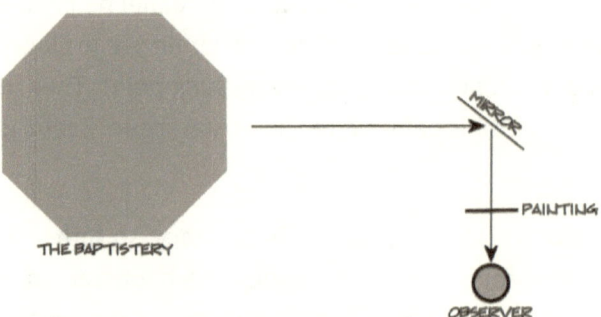

27. The observer looks through the hole in Brunelleschi's painting to see the reflection of the Baptistery in the mirror.

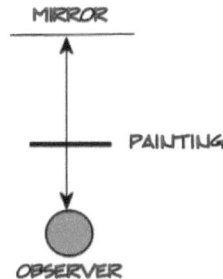

28. The observer then looks through the hole to the mirror which reflects Brunelleschi's painting. (This represents one of several theories as to exactly how Brunelleschi performed his experiment.)

The lengths Brunelleschi went through demonstrates the prime importance of the observational point of view, as regards comparison. Its importance is further emphasized by Alberti in <u>On Painting</u>, as we will see. The point is, in order to judge a work of art against its model, it must be done by looking at each in the same way – from the same *perspective*. The point of view the artist used to create the effect is just as vital as the vanishing point in the effect produced. The vanishing point is contained within the *rendering* of perspective, while the point of observation resides within the artist's *perception* of perspective.

What does Alberti have to say about comparison and viewpoints?

Know that a painted thing can never appear truthful where there is not a definite distance for seeing it. I will give the reason for this if ever I write of my demonstrations which were called miracles by my friends when they saw and marveled at them.

One wonders exactly what Alberti refers to as his 'miraculous demonstrations'. Could it have been something similar to Brunelleschi's? But much more interesting to me is Alberti's assertion which his demonstration would have sought to prove: *a painted thing can never appear truthful where there is not a definite distance for seeing it*. That 'definite distance' is the fixed point of

73

observation needed for observing- and then rendering- perspective accurately.

This makes perfect sense, of course – when painting a picture of something from nature, you don't shift your point of view halfway through. And these laws of optics apply equally whether the model is being observed for a painting or a sculpture. In either case, the most accurate means of visual comparison is to place your live model and your work relative to a single point of observation.

In sculpting using this principle, the visual image of your clay (if accurate) should replicate the visual image of your model. For this to happen, the visual *environments* of the live model and the clay modello need to be identical as well. If you have your live model under one light source and your clay under a different one, or your live model farther away from you (or higher on a tripod, or lower) than your clay work of the same size, they will never appear equal from a single point of observation – *even when they are actually equal*.

The only real difference between observing while painting versus sculpture is that sculptors must periodically rotate their work, as well as their model, for additional angles. As long as the visual relationship between model, clay modello, and viewpoint of the sculptor remain constant from angle to angle, the technique will work.

If you have ever instinctually stepped back several feet from your work in order to judge your progress when sculpting or painting, you have subconsciously intuited the benefits of observation in perspective. This instinct is based in geometry and optics. There exists a 'certain distance' at which you will be able to judge and compare most effectively – close enough to understand detail, far enough away to comprehend the form in its entirety. There even exist points of observation that allows your model and your work to appear to be of equal size, when one is actually of a smaller scale.

This visual relation is one of the more esoteric principles in figurative sculpture. Few sculptors learn of these objective optical principles in art school, though many develop their methods towards these principles, with time and experience.

All knowledge of large, small; long, short; high, low; broad, narrow; clear, dark; light and shadow and every similar attribute is obtained by comparison... Thus all things are known by comparison. For comparison contains within itself a power which immediately demonstrates in objects which is more, less or equal.

In his discussions of observation, Alberti moves on from the science of optics, and touches upon the more subtle nature of perception. The act of comparison when observing, detailed in the quote above, hardly needs explanation. It's worth repeating here, though, to illustrate Alberti's acknowledgement of the power of observation as a tool for rendering nature. Though Alberti never states a preference, I have to wonder whether he and other sculptors of the Early Renaissance placed a preeminence on the "power which immediately demonstrates in objects which is more, less or equal" over the " wonderful, sure strength that is almost unbelievable" (Della Statua, section two) found in Alberti's dimensions and setting of points.

For all its power, observation is necessarily a subjective means of information. The accuracy of Brunelleschi's painting of the Baptistery would fail to astonish in the light of the technology of photography, at least in terms of visual objectivity. But when an artist strives to give his best, most honest attempt to reproduce his visual perception, the degree by which he fails might be hallmark of the artist's true expression and style.

On Sculpture

As subjective as our perception is, and as faulty as our judgment may be, there are means by which an artist can mitigate or overcome these shortcomings in pursuit of accuracy. Alberti mentions several - beginning one's study with simple exercises and progressing into complexities, memory training, repetitive practice, and the close study of nature in all its abundance. Two pieces of advice, further, touch upon observation and perception that are well worth repeating, especially as they have been in common practice with painters and sculptors since the time of Alberti and likely before.

A good judge for you to know is the mirror. I do not know why painted things have so much grace in the mirror. It is marvelous how every weakness in a painting is so manifestly deformed in the mirror. Therefore things taken from nature are corrected with a mirror. I have here truly recounted things which I have learned from nature.

The use of a mirror to identify and correct mistakes in draughtsmanship is still in use today in the studios which practice traditional figurative work. To those who do not know its use, Alberti's advice concerning mirrors may seem confusing. Here's how it works: while standing at your point of observation of the model and the work at hand (it functions equally for drawing, painting, and sculpture), take a small hand mirror, preferably one without a frame, and hold it in front of your face in such a way that you can see your model and your work reversed. The image can be flipped upside down by holding the mirror to your brow, or more commonly it can be reversed left to right by holding the mirror to the side of your nose.

You will have to turn to the side in order to view your work and model, as shown here.

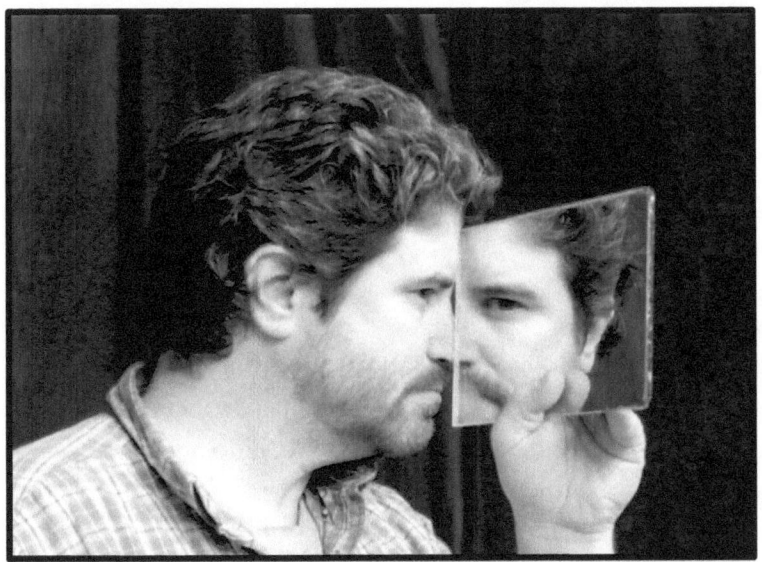

29. What the model sees when the artist uses the mirror to reverse his visual field.

The point of this exercise it to present a 'new' image to your brain. The principle behind this that one hears repeated throughout the studios these days is that your brain gets tired, or at least acclimated, to seeing the same form over and over – so after spending a few hours looking at the same model, your mind gets a bit lazy. In addition, any mistakes that go uncorrected in your work tend to be overlooked, to the point that your mind does not easily recognize them as mistakes. Indeed, after having the mistake in front of your eyes for a period of time, your subconscious begins to 'recognize' it and consider it as correct because it is familiar.

The mirror is the remedy for this. By reversing the visual input, you present to your mind an image that the mind sees as 'new'; mistakes once overlooked now "marvelously" jump right out at you, just as Alberti describes. Many people have had a similar experience after prolonged periods of study or labor of various sorts: who hasn't left off a work in frustration, only to come back to it a day later and have the mistakes seem obvious? The lapse of time does the same thing the mirror does. But rather than waiting a day to see your obstacles, the mirror provides them instantly.

Leonardo Da Vinci, in his own treatise on painting written a half century or so later, also recommends use of the mirror and praising its utility, going so far as to refer the mirror as "the true master of painters."

Alberti's and DaVinci's recommendation to use the mirror to correct mistakes is the tacit acknowledgement of the imperfection of observation. The imperfections of visual method do not arise in the theory, though, but in the practice. The optics and geometry of observation are an objective foundation upon which we artists apply our imperfect, human, subjective talents. This subjectivity is the realm of personal taste and style, as well as a record of the artist's perception of the world.

On the other hand, knowing that our minds are fallible in the observation department, we might also seek aid from mirrors and elsewhere, in order to more fully understand and master the way in which we see.

Jumping back to On Sculpture, we encounter the last line of the book:

Further, those who wish to make this art their profession should know principally the distance of every projection or hollow of any member from a particular disposition of lines.

This non-sequitur last sentence is impossible to understand without reading Alberti's other treatise. What Alberti refers to here is use of a device he describes in On Painting:

Here is a good aid for whoever wishes to make use of it. Nothing can be found, so I think, which is more useful than that veil which among my

78

friends I call an intersection. It is a thin veil, finely woven, dyed whatever color pleases you and with larger threads [marking out] as many parallels as you prefer. This veil I place between the eye and the thing seen, so the visual pyramid penetrates through the thinness of the veil. This veil can be of great use to you.

Like the elements of perspective, the use of a grid to create a replica of an original is known to anyone who ever attended a high school art class. A grid of intersecting lines is drawn on a picture, and a similar grid is drawn on another piece of paper. The contents of each square of the grid present to the artist easily digestible bits of visual information, allowing the artist to transfer the picture one small chunk at a time, and thanks to the grid pattern, each small chunk is put in the correct place.

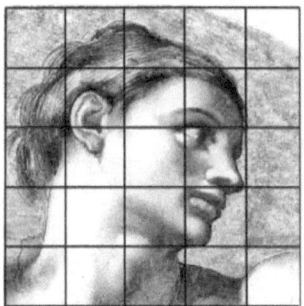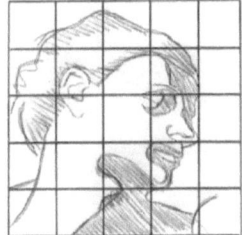

30. A grid drawn on a picture, and a sketch of the same picture produced using a similar grid.

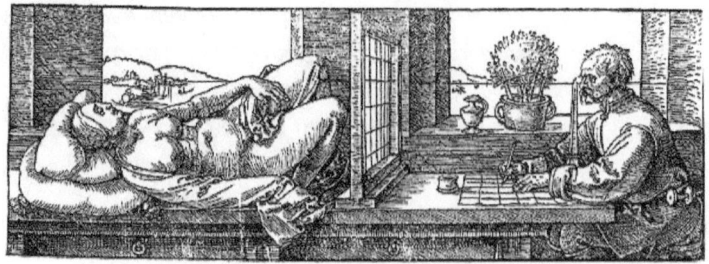

31. An engraving by Albrecht Durer, about 1525.

With Alberti's Veil, though, the grid exists on a transparent plane between the artist and the live model, like a window. This idea caught the imagination of artists, who devised their own similar versions of Alberti's veil, diagrams and sketches of which survive to the present day.

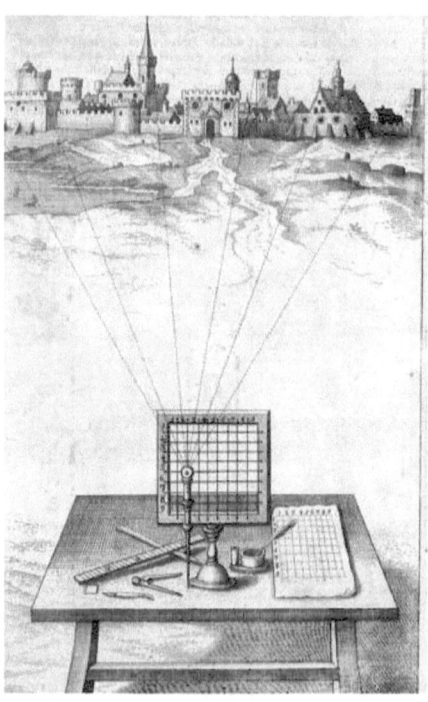

32. Robert Fludd's diagram of Alberti's veil from the early 17th century. Note the eyepiece which stands in a fixed relation to the veil, providing the observational point of view.

Notice that there is a device for locating the eye of the observer – that is, the eye of the artist – in a very precise point. If the model is observed through the grid from any other point of view, the grid provides a faulty reading. Again, we see the vital importance of the point of observation in rendering perspective from nature.

Complexity arises when we try to apply this device to sculpture, as Alberti suggests in his final line. This may be why he chose not to elaborate on it in On Sculpture, though he does at least allude to the complexity in On Painting:

Firstly, it [Alberti's Veil] always presents to you the same unchanged plane... This would certainly be difficult without the intersection. You know how impossible it is to imitate a thing which does not continue to present the same appearance, for it is easier to copy painting than sculpture. You know that as the distance and the position of the centre are changed, the thing you see seems greatly altered. Therefore the veil will be, as I said, very useful to you, since it is always the same thing in the process of seeing. ..

The first issue we encounter with Alberti's Veil applied to sculpture is the necessary mobility of a clay modello in the process of its creation. We rotate the life model to work from a multitude of viewpoints, and we rotate the clay modello accordingly. If either the clay work or the life model are not completely centered on their rotational axes relative to each other, though, they will move away from or closer to each other as they rotate. If the distance between model and modello changes, the observational viewpoint must also change in order to preserve the correct relationship between the three. Therefore, the eyepiece which accompanies Alberti's Veil would need to be reset at every rotation.

Secondly, of course, there is no background on a clay modello upon which we can draw a grid! The only feasible solution would to be use two veils and two observational points of view – one to view the life model and the other to view the clay model. Even then, the sculptor would have to step around to the other side of the clay model's veil to model the clay, and step back to check the work.

81

On Sculpture

These two complexities are not insurmountable, but are highly impractical. However, a studio practice has evolved – whether directly from Alberti's veil, or perhaps from cartography and surveying techniques familiar to architects and builders, it is hard to say – that provides a similar sort of visual guideline akin to the veil. This is the use of the plumbline.

As we have seen with Alberti's Diffinitore, plumblines are useful for creating perfectly straight lines from which measurements may be made. A plumbline is merely a single line taken off Alberti's Veil and held at arm's length. It will always fall plumb – that is its job, after all – and so it can be used to contrast any contour on a model and measure the degree to which that contour varies from 'plumb'. One can also align different parts of a model and compare that alignment on one's work. It's a little like a visual yardstick.

While a plumbline doesn't give you convenient little squares to fill in on a background like the Veil does for painters, it does provide the sculptor with a guide that does not alter from one point of view to the other. Spin the clay modello and the live model all you want; the plumbline will always fall straight. And since there is no grid, there isn't a chance of your work being thrown out of scale if your observational point of view changes slightly, as happens in sculpture when the work rotates. It works just as well for painters and draughtsmen, of course, and for centuries has been standard equipment in the painter's toolbox.

Beyond mirrors and veils, Alberti suggest another aid to the artist's perception of Nature: a second opinion. As Alberti describes in On Painting:

...Therefore, give to things a moderated diligence and take the advice of friends. In painting open yourself to whoever comes and hear everyone. The work of the painter attempts to be pleasing to the multitude; therefore do not disdain the judgment and views of the multitude when it is possible to satisfy their opinions. They say that Apelles hid behind a painting so that

each one could more freely criticize it and so that he could hear their honest opinions: Thus he heard how each one blamed or praised. Hence I wish our painter openly to demand and to hear each one who judges him. This will be most useful to him in acquiring pleasantness. There is no one who does not think it an honor to pass judgment on the labors of others.... Therefore, hear each one, but first of all have everything well thought out and well thrashed out with yourself. When you have heard each one, believe that most expert.

This is the traditional foundation of instruction in the arts, of course – it is known as the critique. Before there were art schools, artists were trained as apprentices by the masters they served. Each made countless mistakes and was in turn corrected by those who possessed knowledge and insight.

With the rise of art schools to replace the master-apprentice relationship, this method of instruction has been weakened. The old system saw a resurgence in the late 20th century, and is commonly now known as the 'atelier' system of education (*atelier* being the French word for 'studio', as the remnants of this educational style descended from the studios of Paris in the late 19th century). However, it could be argued that the generation of painters and sculptors in Alberti's day benefitted from neither the master/apprentice system nor a more formalized education. Donatello, Ghiberti, Brunelleschi were all breaking new ground, and could not rely on the advice of the older generation of masters (most of these artists were trained as goldsmiths, who could offer little advice to large-scale bronze and marble sculptors working from live models). Thus they turned to each other for both correction and reassurance, much in the way Alberti himself, in the dedication of <u>On Painting</u> to Brunelleschi, pleads:

May it please you, then, to read me with diligence. If anything here seems to you to need emending, correct me. There was never a writer so learned to whom erudite friends were not useful.

On Sculpture

Jason Arkles is an American sculptor living and working in Florence, Italy. He studied under Charles Cecil in Florence. Jason concentrates his work upon portraiture and monuments, forgoing galleries and working by private and public commission. In 2010 he opened a teaching atelier, Studio della Statua, named after Alberti's treatise. In addition to this translation of Alberti, Jason has written <u>Sculpting From Life- A studio Manual of the Sight-Size Method</u>, which describes a body of visual techniques historically utilized by painters but which is gaining traction with contemporary figurative sculptors.

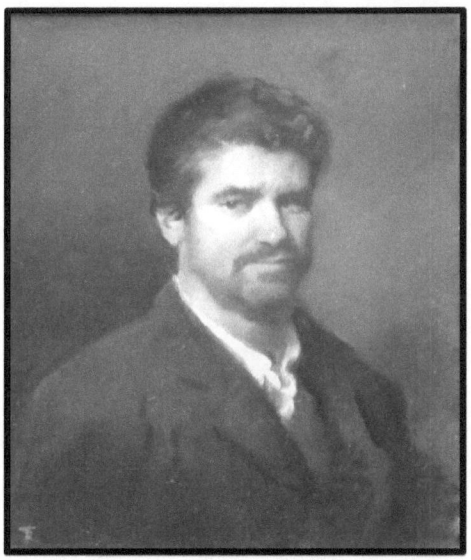

Portrait of Jason Arkles, by Tom Richards.

On Sculpture

www.ingramcontent.com/pod-product-compliance
Lightning Source LLC
Chambersburg PA
CBHW022125170526
45157CB00004B/1755

9 7 8 1 3 0 0 9 6 5 8 5 5